Therapist into coach

***Coaching in Practice* series**

The aim of this series is to help coaching professionals gain a broader understanding of the challenges and issues they face in coaching, enabling them to make the leap from being a 'good-enough' coach to an outstanding one. This series is an essential aid for both the novice coach, eager to learn how to grow a coaching practice, and the more experienced coach looking for new knowledge and strategies. Combining theory with practice, it provides a comprehensive guide to becoming successful in this rapidly expanding profession.

Published and Forthcoming titles:
Rogers: Developing a Coaching Business (2006)
Hayes: NLP Coaching (2006)
Bluckert: Psychological Dimensions of Executive Coaching (2006)
Hay: Reflective Practice and Supervision for Coaches

Therapist into coach

Julia Vaughan Smith

Open University Press

Open University Press
McGraw-Hill Education
McGraw-Hill House
Shoppenhangers Road
Maidenhead
Berkshire
England
SL6 2QL

email: enquiries@openup.co.uk
world wide web: www.openup.co.uk

and Two Penn Plaza, New York, NY 10121–2289, USA

First published 2007

Copyright © Julia Vaughan Smith, 2007

All rights reserved. Except for the quotation of short passages for the purposes of criticism and review, no part of this publication may be reproduced, stored in a retrieval system, or transmitted, in any form, or by any means, electronic, mechanical, photocopying, recording or otherwise, without the prior permission of the publisher or a licence from the Copyright Licensing Agency Limited. Details of such licences (for reprographic reproduction) may be obtained from the Copyright Licensing Agency Ltd of 90 Tottenham Court Road, London, W1T 4LP.

A catalogue record of this book is available from the British Library

ISBN 0 335 22351 9 (pb)   0 335 22052 5 (hb)
ISBN 978 0335 22051 9 (pb)   978 0355 22052 6 (hb)

Library of Congress Cataloging-in-Publication Data
CIP data applied for

Typeset by YHT Ltd, London
Printed in Poland by OZ Graf. S.A. www.polskabook.pl

The **McGraw·Hill** Companies

To Don, for all the reasons he will know.

Contents

	Series preface	ix
	Preface	xi
	Acknowledgements	xiii
1	Getting started	3
2	Becoming a coach	10
3	Coaching: facilitating personal change	18
4	Coaching framework	34
5	Differences between therapy and coaching	45
6	The coaching relationship	53
7	Coaching interventions and techniques	64
8	The coaching process	84
9	Barriers, problems and challenges	111
10	Which coaching market?	124
11	Integrating coaching with other practises	135
	End piece	142
	Bibliography	144
	Index	147

Series preface

The coaching world is expanding. A profession that was largely unknown a decade ago is now an attractive second career for increasing numbers of people looking for new ways of growing their interest in the development of people. Some observers estimate that the number of new coaches joining the market is doubling every year.

Yet while there are many books which cater for the beginner coach, including my own book, also published by Open University Press, *Coaching Skills: A Handbook*, there are relatively few which explore and deepen more specialist aspects of the role. That is the purpose of this series. It is called *Coaching in Practice* because the aim is to unite theory and practice in an accessible way. The books are short, designed to be easily understood, without in any way compromising the integrity of the ideas they explore. All are written by senior coaches with, in every case, many years of hands-on experience.

This series is for you if you are undertaking or completing your coaching training and perhaps in the early stages of the unpredictability, pleasures and dilemmas that working with actual clients brings. Now that you have passed the honeymoon stage, you may have begun to notice the limitations of your approaches and knowledge. You are eager for more information and guidance. You probably know that it is hard to make the leap between being a good-enough coach and an outstanding one. You are thirsty for more help and challenge. You may also be one of the many people still contemplating a career in coaching. If so, these books will give you useful direction on many of the issues which preoccupy, perplex and delight the working coach.

That is where I hope you will find the *Coaching in Practice* series so useful.

One of the hottest topics in coaching is, *what is the difference between coaching and therapy?* This book answers the question from an unusual angle because it is written by someone who is both a qualified, practising therapist and an experienced executive coach. For this reason it will be vital reading for any therapist considering making the transition into coaching. If you are such a therapist, it will reassure you that you already have many of the skills that you will need in order to thrive as a coach. At the same time it will clearly spell out where and how you need to change your attitudes, approaches and behaviours with many practical suggestions for building your skills. The book also has many tried and tested ideas for client-friendly activities to use in a coaching session. This book should also be required reading for coaches who are wondering where the boundaries are with therapy because, although not written with this purpose in mind, it is the clearest explanation I have yet seen of the differences, both large and small, between the two disciplines.

Jenny Rogers

Preface

This book was written as a response to all those psychotherapists and counsellors who have asked me: 'So what really is coaching?', and have said: 'Isn't it what we already do?' It is also a response to those who are sceptical about the value and place of coaching within the field of personal development: 'Isn't it narcissistic and superficial?', or even: 'Isn't it just another way of taking money from people?' Talking to a range of different psychological therapists and other practitioners about coaching has provided many opportunities to explore the place of coaching, its relationship with psychotherapy and counselling, and issues around personal change. All these conversations have informed this book.

During the writing I have ranged across the stereotypes (coaching is superficial/therapy takes too long) as if they were in opposition to each other. Like all stereotypes, there is a small grain of truth and a vast quantity of prejudice and even, perhaps, envy. In reality, there is space for all processes, they don't have to attack or defeat each other; they are not enemies. Coaching is not another way of doing therapy. It is a different process with a different intention. I hope through this book to enable you to get a sense of what coaching brings to personal change, and its value and relevance to the fast-moving world in which we all live.

This isn't an academic book, evaluating the theoretical constructs or research literature. It takes a practical approach for those who want to hear the voice of coaching and to get a picture of how it works. While I haven't used this book to give you a tool kit for coaching, the examples I use illustrate the range of approaches that are applied within a coaching orientation. The examples are drawn from clients and my own experiences as a client and coach, however, they are all made up by me to illustrate the points I hope to get across. They are not accounts of actual client work. All the coaches and clients are fictitious.

Throughout the book I refer to therapists as a grouping, primarily including psychotherapists, counsellors, art therapists, drama therapists and clinical psychologists. I am aware of the wide range of therapeutic and counselling practises within the field on the spectrum of psychoanalytic to humanistic orientations. My aim is to try to speak to you all; at times, that might mean that I am speaking to a particular orientation but, overall, I hope that I am speaking sufficiently to your particular discipline so that you can develop your understanding of the relationship between coaching and your way of working.

I run a mixed practice of Executive and Career Transition Coaching, Psychotherapy and Organizational Consulting. After a career in management, education and training, I worked as an Organizational Development Consultant, then included Executive Coaching in my portfolio. As part of my own personal and career development, I subsequently trained and qualified as an Integrative and Humanistic Psychotherapist. I find working with people in different ways energizing and stimulating. I know that my experience in one practice informs the other, while at the same time I also know that I approach therapy and coaching in different ways. I hope to share some of that experience with you to inform your own developing thoughts about coaching and how it might become part of your work.

Acknowledgements

This book has been crafted from my work with coaching and psychotherapy peers, clients and course participants over a number of years. Without them, there would be little material for me to have worked on. I am grateful to them for enabling me to develop as a coach and write this book. There are some particular people who have helped me in very specific ways, by challenging and shaping my ideas, keeping me focused and enabling me to complete this project. They include my friend Jane Krish, whose time and interest I very much appreciated and Valerie Iles, whose ideas on strategy, complexity and partnership have added to my practice. Also Jan Campbell-Young and Caroline Sanford-Wood, colleagues in coaching and coach training, who with Laurence Jarosy, were willing to read and comment on the drafts. I would also like to thank my Australian friend and colleague, Brian Lewis for demonstrating powerful questions so effectively. Everyone who has asked me 'how the writing is going' has helped me move it along. Despite all this great support and input from so many people, nothing would be published without Don Oldham's dedicated time spent taming my writing and without Jenny Rogers' guidance and belief. Thank you all.

Preparatory exercise

Before you start reading this book, I suggest you just take a bit of time to think about why coaching and why now? We ask our clients at their first session: 'What brings you to coaching?' As this is a coaching book, perhaps it is a good question for you to think about too.

What has brought you to read this book? Perhaps you have heard about coaching and are curious, or are you looking for some change in direction for yourself? Maybe you have been practising as a psychological therapist for some time and want to take on something different, something that uses many of the same skills but within a different framework. Perhaps you are finding the weekly commitment to clients, common in most therapies, limiting and would like to get a bit more freedom in your life. As with many clients coming into coaching, maybe you are in a transition, with some things ended and not sure what the new beginnings might be. Perhaps you are sceptical and want to have some assumptions confirmed or denied.

- So, why this book and why now? What is going on in your life, professional and personal, that may be motivating you to pick up this book?
- What are you hoping for from this book? What is it that you want to get out of reading it?
- What might you need to do to be sure of getting the most that you possibly can from it?

Take some time to reflect on these coaching questions before you turn the page.

1 Getting started

> The important thing is to know how to begin.
>
> Henry Moore

As well as coaching individuals, I also run training programmes for people who want to become coaches or those who want to include coaching skills within their management practice. We start many of these training programmes with a session about what coaching is, and find that people have a range of different ideas and images, arising from the different ways in which the term coach or coaching is used. Often, too, consultancy or therapy practitioners respond to discussions on coaching with: 'I'm not sure if what I am doing is coaching or not.' Both of these responses were mine when I started coaching 15 or so years ago. At that time, coaching was gaining momentum in the USA and was being picked up within the field of leadership and management development, where I was then working. I became interested in coaching because of its potential to enable people to move forward, to develop and improve their life. As a process, I felt it had much to offer and that has been my repeated experience working with many clients. As coaching has developed, there is increasing evidence that the approach does enable people to make and sustain change in their life and, within organizational settings, to improve their effectiveness and achievement. The power of coaching is seen and felt on the first encounter and for most, is an entirely positive and motivating experience. This is encouraging and enlivening for the coach as much as the client.

Coaching offers psychological therapists another way of working with people and their development on a one-to-one basis. As it is not another way of doing therapy, it offers an opportunity to step back from the emotional challenges and certain restrictions a therapeutic process may bring. The nature of the work and the coaching relationships can provide a freer way of working that therapists can find liberating. I've used the term coaching a number of times in these opening paragraphs and maybe this is a good point to define what I mean by it. I use coaching to refer to a way of working one-to-one, or with a team, with the purpose of achieving personal development and change. Coaching is a future-focused, goal- and action-orientated process that uses many of the same skills as therapy but within a different orientation and relationship.

The term coaching may be used to describe a more formal process between a coach and a client. Coaching is also used to mean an approach and a set of skills that can be used in any setting. For example, at work, you might use a coaching approach with a colleague or member of staff to facilitate personal or work related development.

The coaching process is one that encourages empowerment; the sense that we can influence what happens in our life as a result of accessing our inner creative resourcefulness. It stimulates high levels of motivation and the will to make the chosen changes, and attends to the skills needed for goal achievement. Coaching enables the people being coached to shift their perceptions, assumptions and ideas of what is possible. I refer to this model of coaching as non-content personal coaching.

Coaching is a process and the coach has expertise in applying that process. As a result, a coach can work with people in many different contexts and with the whole range of issues that individuals might wish to resolve through coaching. Coaches are proactive, that is, they are fully involved in the process. Coaches are also non-directive, that is, as the coach, you won't be giving advice, guidance or engaging in other forms of telling clients what they should do.

In this way it differs from the model it is most often linked with – sports coaching – where coaches may take up the position of instructor/trainer with the aim of getting the most potential out of athletes by establishing a training regime and improving their technique. Other variations on this model might include drama, voice or business coaching, where there is a training and instruction component to the work, and the coach has specific expertise in that area. This is a valid form of working and may use many of the same coaching skills and interventions, but it isn't the model I am referring to in this book.

Coaching, as a practice, is expanding rapidly as individuals and organizations feel its value and benefits. This expansion perhaps reflects the challenges of change that are part of life and the increasing number of options, possibilities and pressures on us. Clients come to coaching when they are stuck, or overwhelmed by options and want to further their personal development. They may also come because they have an exciting idea and want help to put it into action.

Life coaching, performance or executive coaching and career coaching

As coaching expands, it is becoming focused on particular markets or niches. The three terms most commonly used are life coaching, executive coaching and career coaching.

The term *life coaching* is sometimes used to reflect the holistic nature of coaching; that is, that it addresses personal, non-work, and work aspects of the client's world. To that extent, all non-content personal coaching is life coaching. Executive and career coaching are also holistic, while providing a particular focus to the coaching. For example, managers in organizations or their own businesses may look to an executive coach because their presenting needs may involve work or business related issues. Alternatively, someone might contact a career coach if the presenting need is a career change or advancement. The coaching would be holistic as these coaches would be working in the belief that work and non-work issues can only be explored together.

Those who describe themselves as *executive coaches* are stating that they have some experience in working with people who hold managerial and leadership roles in organizations and with the complexities and pressures that go with those roles. This focus to the coaching is also sometimes called performance coaching, where the clients' performance at work is part of what they want to improve.

A *career coach* will have decided to place the focus on issues connected with career transition and transformation, having worked in a related field before, for example, in human resources, education or training.

Increasingly, those at the top of organizations, for example, those holding director level and managerial roles are turning to coaching to work on their personal, professional and career development. As part of that, they may also choose to address issues of their work/life balance. Coaching provides a trusted person, who is outside of the organization, and with whom things can be explored in total confidence. Being in a senior position in a company can be a lonely place and the coaching relationship offers a valuable opportunity to talk about things that are, perhaps, not going well. It is a place where people can talk about their struggles and difficulties and find ways to resolve them. For many this is not possible within the culture of their organization, where admitting fears or lack of skills and insight is not accommodated and, in fact, can be seen as career-limiting. Coaching is used by employers, to provide personal and role development for staff who are known to be underachieving or struggling. It is also used to help high fliers prepare for their next role.

The three broad groupings of life, executive and career coaching are further differentiated into business coaching, leadership coaching, performance coaching, relationship coaching and into specialist areas such as giving up smoking coaching, weight loss coaching, and anxiety coaching. All these approaches could use the same model of non-content coaching. Specializing in this way as a non-content coach means having a tailored tool kit of exercises that helps clients with particular needs who come to coaching. The coach will also have relevant experience and knowledge as an internal resource to bring to the work, and will draw on this to add ideas to those created by the client, while continuing to be non-directive.

There are also people working in the fields of life coaching and work-based (performance, business or leadership) coaching, who call themselves coaches, and who use a coaching model involving instruction and tuition, in which case, the coach is proactive and directive. This model works well where clients want to develop particular skills or behaviour. For example, if they want to improve their interview skills, it may be beneficial to be taken through a coaching-training process to learn different skills. It can also be beneficial, where coaches have specific expertise that they use to underpin the process. For example, in giving up smoking, where there is a combination of coaching expertise with content knowledge. In some of my executive and career coaching work, I do at times take up a coaching-training role in those areas where I have particular expertise, if that is what the client wants. For areas where I don't have expertise, I explore with clients their thoughts on getting the skills development they need.

There are also coaches who differentiate themselves by their psychological, or psycho-social, orientations. For example, some coaches offer psychological coaching or gestalt coaching. In so doing, they are identifying that they bring a particular approach to the coaching. A gestalt coach would, for example, bring his or her gestalt framework to the coaching process. These coaches may use aspects of their particular theoretical base to inform the coaching process through the exercises they use.

The coaching client

As with all personal development and change processes, clients need to be willing participants. They come to coaching saying things like:

> I've got this big job and I really want to succeed in it and keep my non-work life in balance.

> I know what I want to do, and I'm really excited about it, I'm just not sure how I am going to make it happen.

> I am finding all these changes so difficult and I feel I have lost myself somehow.

> I feel really stuck, I know I need to make some changes but I just can't see a way forward.

What tends to attract clients to coaching is that it is a focused process that is different from counselling and psychotherapy. They sometimes say: 'I don't want just to sit and talk about how I am feeling, I want to focus and move forward' or 'I don't want to talk about my childhood, I want to talk about the future.' In effect, they are choosing to stay primarily 'in the light' of their external life, and their responses to what life demands and offers, rather than enter into the darker areas, 'beneath ground', of their fantasies and internalized experience. They are saying that they do not want therapy but do want a developmental process.

Most people come into coaching at a time of transition, either enforced, 'My company is moving to Scotland and I am just not sure if I want to go with them', or arrived at personally. Often a phase of life has ended or they have lost motivation for what they are currently doing in their life. What they experience when looking forward is anxiety, limitation or blankness. Others have a sense of what they would rather have but keep sabotaging themselves by telling themselves: 'I'll fail'; 'People will think I've really lost it' or 'They wouldn't take me on.' Clients may come to coaching if they feel they are failing to achieve things or know they are under-performing. They may also come to coaching if they sense they have made a wrong decision, for example, taken a job or moved to a different area and things haven't turned out the way they hoped.

As with therapy and counselling, people of all ages, from all walks of life and from a wide range of cultures come to coaching. They will often do so hoping that the coach will tell them what to do, or give them advice, just as they can get from therapy. Clients might bring small or large issues to coaching and will move at different paces as regards their readiness to make changes.

Coaching clients have decided they don't want to go down a therapeutic route and are sufficiently able to plan and propel themselves into the future. Clients who come to coaching tend not to want to work on psycho-emotional experience, usually because they do not have a sense of themselves as being adversely affected by the impact of life events. Clients are unlikely to come to coaching to seek help to work through and accommodate traumatic experiences, troubling feelings and behaviour or relational disturbances. Clients who are affected in these ways turn to therapy where they can get the appropriate support.

Mentoring, consultancy and supervision

Mentoring, consultancy and supervision are related to, but clearly differentiated from, coaching, although they may use a similar approach and many of the same skills. A mentor is usually someone with experience and expertise in the field in which the client works or aspires to work.

For example, Sue is an artist who wants to establish herself and sell more of her work. She met Stephen professionally at an event; he is already established in Sue's field of art and is well respected for his work and for how he has created his business. Sue liked him and asked if he would become her mentor; someone she could talk to on a regular basis about her work and business, and who would give her advice, based on his experience. The relationship between Sue and Stephen isn't a financial one and they may talk on the phone or meet up at a café or over lunch. Stephen is a good listener; he asks Sue probing and powerful questions, and reflects on the things that have helped him and what he notices about the business. Mentoring has its origins within the 'master practitioner' and 'journeyman' concepts of apprenticeship and is known to have a positive benefit for those who wish to advance their career in a particular field. The mentors pass on their knowledge, experience, wisdom and insights to their 'mentees', who can use that to develop their career. Mentors might also open doors by, for example, putting their mentees in contact with people who might be able to help or further advise them. Some coaches step into a mentoring role if that is to the benefit of the client. For example, where the coach has specific information or experience that might be valuable to the client and where withholding it would be an odd and possibly a punitive thing to do. The important thing, within coaching, is not to limit clients' opportunity to develop their own resourcefulness while at the same time not withholding information that might be of value. Part of coaching, supervision or reflective practice, is to manage this boundary and to ensure that the coach isn't falling into the 'telling and advising' mode of working. If clients need some advice and guidance, there are likely to be more useful people than coaches to give it to them, people with more relevant experience. Within a coaching relationship you might, as the coach, put forward the idea of getting a mentor if your client has a goal regarding career development. If it were an idea that feels useful to the client, you would work together to identify possible mentors and to establish a mentoring relationship with someone who feels most appropriate to the client.

A consultant is a kind of mentor. Usually consultants bring an outside view to a situation, together with expertise and a specialty focus. For example, an organizational development consultant will have an expertise in organizational psychology, group dynamics, strategic frameworks and other related fields; and an IT consultant will have specialist expertise in a particular part of information technology. Consultants will use some of the same skills as coaching. Consultancy is, however, a different practice as it can be directive, and usually involves giving advice and guidance.

Supervision may use many of the same skills as coaching. However, the purpose and context of the work are different. In most approaches to supervision, including therapy and coaching supervision, there is an aspect of the work that will involve the supervisor carrying some shared advocacy for the client's clients as well as for the development of the therapist. There is often an element of mentoring within the relationship as well, and at times supervisors give advice and guidance that are valuable aspects to the supervisory relationship. Their role includes coaching, mentoring, professional development and the maintenance of professional standards. They have a vested interest in the professional practice of their clients.

The receiver of the coaching is usually referred to as the client, sometimes as the coachee. Where managers use coaching with their staff, they tend to use the term 'coachee' for the person being coached to differentiate the relationship from that of a more formal coach and client. Throughout this book I refer to *the client* as you are likely to be working mostly with paying clients and it best denotes the nature of the relationship. However, that is personal choice and the terms are synonymous.

I am addressing the ideas in this book to a wide and varied field of those who practice within psychotherapy and counselling. While being aware of the debates within this field on the differences and similarities between psychotherapy and counselling, and between different orientations, I use the generic term of *therapist* throughout.

2   Becoming a coach

Why do you want to become a coach? Maybe you are thinking that you could take on coaching clients as well as, or instead of, your therapy or counselling clients. For example, it may be that you want some variety in your work, to have a greater degree of flexibility or to increase your earnings. You may decide to run a mixed practice or to move away from therapy altogether. Adopting a different way of practising requires internal and external changes. You will also need to think about the coaching market on which you are going to focus.

Reasons therapists tend to move to coaching

There are several reasons that draw therapists to an interest in coaching and the decision to develop as a coach. You might find that you identify with one or more of these; they are not mutually exclusive.

Positive approach

You may want to work with a different range of clients and to experience some release from the distress and disturbance that clients can bring into the therapy relationship. Therapy often requires us to listen to the dark and violent aspects of human nature and behaviour and to work with the consequences suffered by clients. Listening to the depths of human despair, and the challenges to therapy that result from it, can take its toll on therapists. You may wish to work with clients where this isn't the central aspect of the process and be able to balance or replace it with the more positive approach associated with coaching. Doing so can be refreshing. You may be feeling burnt out after many years as a therapist and just need a change. Coaching uses so many of the skills that therapists have, that it can offer a valuable alternative and/or complementary practice.

Expanding a service

You may already work in a setting, for example, a counselling service within an institution such as a university or hospital, and recognize that coaching offers an additional service that you could provide. This could result in your being able to support the personal development of staff and at the same time increase the level of contacts to your service. This might bring variety and locate your service differently. For example, counselling services can be marginalized within an organization, and being able to provide coaching can result in employees viewing the service more positively. Not only employees perhaps, but also those who make the funding decisions that support the finances allocated to your service.

Potential to increase income

Another reason therapists are drawn to coaching is in the hope of being able to increase their level of earnings. Therapy tends to be under-valued within society and therapists often work with people on limited incomes. Therapists often see themselves as part of the charitable or voluntary sector, by which I mean providing a public service for a low fee. They are less likely to see themselves as being in business nor do they tend to market their services specifically to those with a higher income. In some areas the competition is high and it is hard to generate sufficient referrals, including self-referrals, to maintain a full-time practice. As a result, it can be hard for therapists in private practice to earn a sufficient income through therapy alone. The expanded market that coaching can offer, together with the potential increase in fees charged can therefore be attractive.

Demand

Some clients expressly state that they don't want to dwell on the past or their their feelings and would prefer strategies and solutions to help move them forward. Some therapy approaches can interpret this as a resistance to engage with their feelings. In this case, therapists might proceed to encourage clients to work with their feelings and their developmental psychology. In some instances, these clients do not stay in therapy after an initial period. They are asking for something from the therapist, which the therapist may not be willing to offer. However, as a therapist, you may want to have an alternative approach to offer clients who ask to work in a particular way. As that work progresses, it may turn out that there are psycho-emotional issues that need a therapeutic process. It may be coaching, however, that makes that more possible for them. Coaching might provide the bridge from resistance to engagement.

Career change

Some people are attracted to coaching as a possible career change. This could be because of early retirement, redundancy, a change in circumstances or wanting a different work/life balance. For example, mental health workers or those working in educational support or similar roles who have had counselling or therapy training, recognize the transferability of many of their skills to coaching. Combining this with a coaching qualification – which could be accomplished within 12 months[1] – makes a career shift a feasible option. Most non-therapists come into coaching out of a desire for a career change and the routes by which people become qualified are varied, as they are for therapy. Working as a coach can be a full-time practice with many of the same issues as for full-time therapy, for example, the need to generate sufficient referrals and contacts to provide the required level of income. It can also be part of a portfolio career, combined with whatever other activities you want to pursue for your own fulfilment or family commitments. Coaching can provide a useful income for you if you want to choose when, and for how many hours, you want to work. You can of course also choose if you want it to be paid or unpaid work.

Coaching, like other practises, is subject to the market forces of demand and competition. It takes energy and commitment to build up a coaching practice. However, it can offer a valuable addition or alternative to your current work and its flexibility means that you can fit it into the life you want to lead.

Becoming a coach is both an internal and an external process. The internal process concerns the development of your ability to step into the coaching frame. To this end, you will need to add coaching skills to your existing therapy skills. You will also have the opportunity to apply some of the techniques and exercises you currently use as a therapist to coaching and develop your competence in using a wide range of coaching interventions. The external process involves you being recognized by others as a coach, for example, through accreditation or membership of a professional body, the establishment of a coaching practice and, possibly, by running a mixed practice.

Internal process in becoming a coach: beliefs, motivation and skill

Depending on your current orientation and practice as a therapist you may need to shift some of your beliefs. For example, you need to be able to believe in the potential power of coaching; that personal change is possible using this process and that you have the resources you need to practice differently. You may already have identified many similarities, shared practises and skills, between your orientation and that of coaching. All your resources and experience as a therapist are valuable, you will, though need to work with them differently within a coaching orientation.

Motivation

The starting point is to explore what your own goals might be as a potential coach. What is it about your current practice that you would like to be different? What would working as a coach have to give you? In what ways could coaching enable you to live out your values? What is it about coaching that might be fulfilling for you? How might coaching fit into the life you want for yourself? Having reflected on these questions and tested out your own level of motivation, you are ready to think about how you might go about achieving these goals.

Developing your coaching skills

Many therapists say to me: 'Surely coaching is what we already do?' My response is usually: 'Coaching uses similar skills but coaching is not therapy.' There is a need, therefore, to invest in developing your coaching skills and orientation. Even where the skills are the same, you are using them in a different framework. You may find it helpful to get some coaching for yourself, to experience it as a client, in the same way you might have done when you trained as a therapist. You could use coaching to support you in achieving the practice transformation you are seeking.

Ladder of learning

Learning any new practice involves a move through a number of developmental stages. Figure 2.1 shows the ladder of learning in all its stages. The first stage is when you are not aware of what you can't do. For example, you are not aware that you do not have all the competences you need for coaching. The second stage – as you practice, get feedback from your clients and reflect

Unconscious incompetence
↓
Conscious incompetence
↓
Conscious competence
↓
Unconscious competence

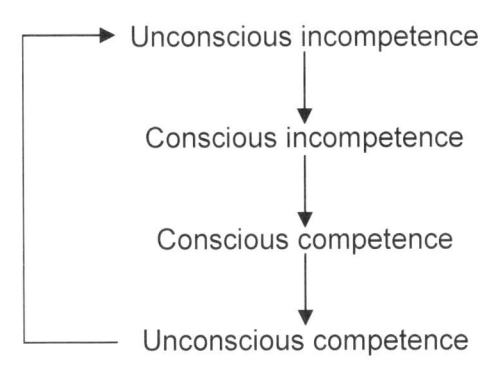

Figure 2.1 Ladder of learning

on your interventions – is that of conscious incompetence, when you are fully aware of where you fall short. Further practice, feedback and reflection will shift this to conscious competence. In this stage you bring all your awareness to bear to ensure you are keeping to the coaching frame and orientation. With even more practice, you will move into unconscious competence, when you don't have to think about it and your interventions and processes flow freely. Even in this stage it is important to continue with personal development, feedback and reflective practice, otherwise unconscious competence can revert to unconscious incompetence.

All learning that involves application goes through these phases, from riding a bike through to any complex set of skills like psychotherapy, counselling and coaching. You may remember the feelings associated with these stages from your previous training. You may only have to think about learning to swim or drive a car, and the level of concentration you needed to bring all of the skills together effectively, to remember this process.

The hardest stage for many is that of conscious incompetence; when you know you are forgetting things or doing things that aren't within a coaching frame. It is at this stage when your own self-limiting beliefs and negative self-talk tend to arise and it is easy to give up the struggle. It can also be at this stage that anxieties and fears arise, for example, the thought that: 'I will forget how to do therapy if I learn how to do coaching.' As with learning any new process, you don't forget what you already know or lose your unconscious competence as long as you continue using those skills. You may fear that you will slip into coaching mode with a therapy client. Would that be so awful? If you found yourself doing that and it caused a disturbance in the work, you would deal with that in the same way as you would for any other disjuncture.

It's the same for clients who want to learn new skills and habits as part of achieving their goals. It can be helpful sometimes to work with them about their own coping strategies for managing this process and not getting disheartened. For example, you might suggest that they bring to mind a previous experience of learning, and then to use that to reflect on what helped them the most. You could then invite them to think about whether any of those strategies or experiences would help them in their present situation. This might be a useful exercise to do yourself.

There are three aspects that are core to developing along this ladder of learning. These are: practice, feedback and reflection. We all need practice, feedback on our practice and opportunities for reflection, either through supervision or on our own (figure 2.2). You have options about how you get these. For example, you could practice on clients, paying or not, or with colleagues, perhaps those who are also developing their competence as a coach. You could also practice the skills whenever an opportunity arises in conversation with friends or colleagues. There are many opportunities every

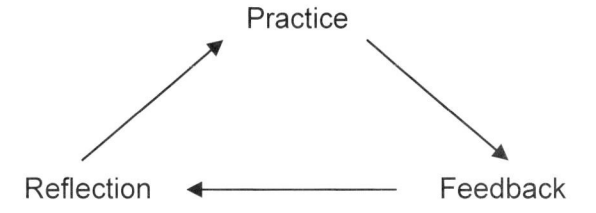

Figure 2.2 Aspects of coaching

day to practice powerful questions and to develop your coaching language. Practising with paying clients can bring additional pressures for a novice coach and it is often helpful to practice with other novice coaches first. This will enable you to get feedback and can also be better for the client. You will need to move into seeing clients in a more formal way, so that you can practice setting up and managing the coaching relationship, and work with a coaching package. As the saying goes: 'You can't learn to swim by standing on dry land.' You have to jump in and practice in a more formal setting. When you start working with clients you will also get feedback from them. Your reflection and practice development will be enhanced, as it is within therapy, through working with a supervisor.

Qualifications, training and legal framework

Like therapy, the routes into coaching are varied. Unlike some therapy training, however, you can gain a Diploma in Coaching within a year, subject to fulfilling the qualification requirements including coaching client hours. You can also do a Master's level degree in two years. Coaches who work in organizational settings or as career coaches tend to be accredited to use a range of valid and reliable personality and psychometric instruments. Many people undertake associated training, for example, in NLP (neuro-linguistic programming), applied Transactional Analysis (TA) or in the use of guided imagery.

At present there are no specific qualification requirements for coaches. You can, therefore, set up as a coach as soon as you feel competent. However, there are many advantages to going through systematic training and having the support of such a programme as you develop your practice. If you want to coach in organizational settings, you will find it beneficial to have a qualification from a recognized provider or awarding body. Organizations are more likely to ask you for evidence of your training and experience. If you plan to see self-referring and paying clients in private practice, that market may deem your qualification as a psychological therapist sufficient in the absence of a formal coaching qualification.

It is probable in the future, that coaches will be expected or even required, to have a relevant qualification and training in coaching. You would be wise, therefore, to keep a detailed record of all coaching and related training, client and supervision hours. If you have this, you are more likely to be able to have your experience accredited when it becomes necessary. You also need to ensure in your advertising that clients can be confident that you are able to work with them effectively.

Becoming a member of an appropriate professional body for coaching, such as the European Mentoring and Coaching Council (EMCC) or to a coaching branch of a therapy or counselling organization, provides your clients with reassurance that you work to a given standard and code of ethics. Clients then have a body to approach if they are dissatisfied with your work or if you have breached the code of ethics. Belonging to such an organization locates you within the coaching world and keeps you up-to-date with coaching developments. Some training organizations, such as the Association for Coaching, fulfil a similar function for their graduates.

As a therapist, you will be familiar with working to a code of ethics or code of conduct. The codes for coaching share many similarities with those for therapy. For example, coaches must ensure they are able to practice at a suitable level of competence, demonstrate evidence of continuing professional development, have appropriate levels of supervision, and recognize when referral is necessary. The codes of ethics also cover issues regarding conflicts of emotional or commercial interest, integrity and honesty, confidentiality and the disclosure of information, acting within the law, not exploiting the client financially, sexually or in any other way and acting in a professional manner. All of which will be familiar to you as part of the code of practice set out by your therapy professional body. Giving a copy to your clients can reassure them that you are a professional practitioner.

One aspect of this code of practice is that you do not mislead your clients and that you are competent to work as a coach. You need to think about how you will present yourself to clients as a novice. Many therapy training programmes accommodate this by arranging for trainees to take on low cost clients who are informed explicitly that the therapist is in training. As a coach, you could take a similar approach by offering free or low cost coaching to individuals or to organizations. This might give you useful experience of working within organizational settings; it would benefit the organization and would not mislead the clients.

Client notes hold the same information as for therapy; that is they form a record with the client's name on and they have the right to ask to see it at any time. Most coaches do not keep extensive notes; they record the goals and the actions for future reference. They might also record the exercises used. As for therapy, coaches have to hold in mind the possibility that a court might subpoena their notes, should there ever be a court case involving the client. You may keep your own reflective record in the same way as you might for your therapy work.

You need to have professional indemnity for this work, in just the same way as for therapy. If you are working in organizations, it is important that you have a signed formal contract for the work that protects you should a complaint arise.

Note

1   Awarding bodies differ as to the length of training and the number of clients and client hours trainees will be expected to fulfil.

3 Coaching
Facilitating personal change

> You can't solve a problem with the same mindset that created it.
> Albert Einstein

Coaching is a process of personal change and development. People don't need to have huge problems to benefit from coaching; on the other hand, coaching can enable people to respond to significant and protracted life issues. Having had coaching, clients say things like:

> It enabled me to make real change, changes that I was afraid would never be possible.

> It's a way to work through what you want for yourself.

> It helped me take the steps I'd been afraid of up to now.

> I learnt about me and how I was limiting what I believed I was capable of.

> It shifted the way I see things, I really thought I only had two choices: to stay or go.

> It enabled me, for the first time, to accept my abilities and achievement, to feel that I was worth something.

> Wow! It helped me change my life. Without it, I am sure I would still be stuck and miserable but telling myself that's what I had to settle for.

The changes that they refer to are both internal and external. That is, coaching results in changes in the beliefs, assumptions, perceptions, thoughts and associated feelings held by clients *and* in changes within their external world, for example, in their career, relationships and work/life balance. The coaching process results in change through using the power of clients' imagination and through challenging the thoughts that limit what they see as

COACHING: FACILITATING PERSONAL CHANGE

Figure 3.1 Individual core thoughts

- Clients' sense of themselves, what gives them meaning and satisfaction
- Negative thoughts, beliefs and perceptions that limit the amount of fulfilment they have achieved
- What the clients would rather have, that would give them a greater sense of fulfilment

possible. It uses a positive approach by looking at solutions, not problems, and by reframing negative thinking.

Coaching works with the three broad aspects of individuals. That is, their core sense of themselves and what matters to them, what they would rather have that would give them a greater sense of fulfilment than they are currently experiencing and the negative thoughts that are stopping them from achieving that greater sense of meaning (figure 3.1).

The coaching orientation works with these beliefs, perceptions and assumptions that are acting as blockages. These will have been developed in response to life experience and result from introjections (those things we have taken in from those around us and scripts given to us). Coaching does not seek to bring about change to those scripts or introjections through working directly with memory or internalized experience. Coaching processes are based on the theory that people can change their behaviour, beliefs, thoughts and attached feelings without needing to understand all of the components. Nor do they need to identify the causal factors or re-experience a situation before a resolution can begin. As such, it is a cognitive-behavioural orientation, which will differ from some therapy practises. Therapists who are practised in cognitive-behavioural therapy, solution-focused therapies or motivational interviewing will find much within coaching that is familiar to them.

Coaching is a humanistic practice. That is, it shares many of the premises of humanistic therapies in that it rejects the medical model, where the therapist is the expert, with the process being that of diagnosis and treatment. Nor is it a psychoanalytical model, where the therapist is the interpreter of the client's experience. Humanistic processes consider the client and coach or therapist as co-workers, jointly engaged in the project of the client's life. As a coach, you will also work in a person-centred way, with empathy and positive regard remaining crucial to the process.

Coaching also draws on the human motivation fields within behavioural and organizational psychology. It uses many of the approaches identified as necessary for motivation. For example, the future- and goal-focus with the sense of reward when the result of hard work is felt to be sufficiently valuable to make the effort to change worthwhile. Coaching also incorporates the belief that personal development, through learning and experience, results in us accessing previously untapped and potential resources that we can use to create a differently satisfying life.

One of the reasons why coaching is being taken up by more and more people is perhaps because life brings so many challenges that people want to develop their capacity to overcome what they perceive to be barriers and to navigate their way through change. In some ways too, it might be a sign of a more affluent society where we are able to ask questions of ourselves, of what we would like life to be like. One of the comments sometimes made about coaching by those who haven't experienced it, is that it fosters a narcissistic approach to life: one of having it all. The charge is that it is seen to be about fostering greed and unrealistic expectations. This is not my experience of coaching, nor of what my clients have wanted from the process: clients are realistic. They know they can't have everything and they don't want success on the back of others' failure. They also know that they can't control the future and they don't want to. What they want is to be able to influence how their life develops by making different choices and finding ways of creating a life that has meaning and better matches their values. If coaching were about fostering self-obsession or unrealistic expectations, it would in my view, be strengthening clients' psychological defence systems but that is not the purpose of coaching.

There is also an analytic approach, discussed in *The Culture of Narcissism* (1979) by Christopher Lasch, which interprets the concept of personal growth as a euphemism for survival: a desire to escape stagnation and death. Such an approach may also interpret the desire for fulfilment as the longing for a state of bliss: an escape from reality. Some people may take a therapeutic or spiritual route as a way of dealing with the challenge to the anxiety of death that's embedded in life. Others come to coaching to find a way of coping with the transient nature of employment, the demands and expectations on them and the changing family environment. It is about surviving the modern conditions that society brings. That seems like a reasonable motivation. At the same time, clients are not looking for a state of bliss. They are realistic.

Coaching is, therefore, an integration of cognitive-behavioural/solutions-focused/positive psychology approaches together with a motivational theory within a humanistic tradition. It is an empowering process, in that the clients realize that they have options and can change things, including their beliefs. They learn that these beliefs are constructs and not the truth. The sense of empowerment also comes from having their talents and strengths affirmed, and their desire for change taken seriously.

Coaching can be a powerful process, in that, done well, it can bring about aspects of internal and external change in a relatively short time. Each session can result in achieving some change in thinking, beliefs and behaviour.

For personal change to be possible within a coaching orientation, clients need to be sufficiently able to do the following:

- engage with a sense of fulfilment;
- take responsibility for themselves;
- create wishes and possibilities;
- draw on a sense of agency to propel themselves into the future;
- develop whatever skills they may need to achieve the goals they set;
- make decisions;
- take action; and
- learn from action and experience.

Engage with a sense of fulfilment

Coaching works with the concept of fulfilment and what that means for individual clients. In doing so, the process engages with what is important to clients, those things that really matter to them and enable them to feel energized and alive. It does this in the belief that if clients can build more of those things into their life, they will experience a deeper sense of enrichment and be in a better position to access more of their potential. Coaching seeks to help clients achieve a better match between the 'what' of their life and those things that matter to them.

In the first or second session with your clients, as the coach, you will offer them an exercise that will enable these things, often referred to in coaching books as *values* and *drivers*, to be explored. For example, David is coaching Simon and using a specific coaching exercise:

> DAVID (COACH): As we start working on what you would like to be different, I'd like to suggest that we spend a bit of time, now, finding out what things really matter to you so that we can be sure that any goals you set enable you to engage fully with them.

Simon agrees to this suggestion.

> DAVID: Find yourself a comfortable sitting position and try to relax. I'm going to suggest that you bring an experience into your awareness in the way that works best for you. You may find it helpful to close your eyes as you do this but it is also okay not to. So, bring into your awareness a memory of a time when things felt really good for you, when you had a sense of being engaged with something that mattered deeply to you and you felt you were

using all of your potential. This could be from any aspect or time of your life. Just let your memories emerge.

David leaves a bit of time for Simon to bring this thought into his mind.

DAVID: Have you thought of a time like this?

SIMON: Yes, it's a time when I was at teacher training college and on teaching practice.

DAVID: Tell me all about it. As you do that, I'm just going to jot down a few words.

SIMON: Well, I was in my mid-twenties and had changed career. I was training to teach drama, art and English within middle schools, you know they were for 8–13-year-olds. I was on placement in a primary school and working with a class of 9-year-olds. Part of my work was to do an integrated teaching project with them, bringing together art, drama and English. It was just great, they made masks, wrote and read fabulous stories, and made up plays. It was fun and everyone was included. They produced some highly creative work. I still have some of it, and that was over 20 years ago. It was really good, I felt alive.

DAVID: (noting the energy in Simon's voice): What was so good about it for you?

SIMON: It was a bit risky, I didn't really know how it would turn out but did a lot of preparation. They were not stuffy lessons, where children had to sit down and behave, I hated all that. They could move around, be free, express themselves and learn something at the same time. It was creative and the children could be involved in different ways. Those who wanted to write could, others did a small bit of writing but more art work, or spontaneously told a story through drama. I just wish I had recorded it all but that would have changed things. I was freed up. We had great things to put on the wall. It was expressive. Just thinking about it makes me feel excited. Of course, in retrospect I can see lots of things that weren't rosy about it that I wasn't aware of at the time, being young and optimistic.

DAVID (who can hear Simon about to bring in some negative thinking): What did you learn from it for yourself?

SIMON: I learnt I could teach in a freer and more creative way; that integrating things works for me and that bringing energy into things really aids learning. I felt proud of what happened. I think the freedom of youth was good, too, not carrying too much angst about doing it right. It felt that I had provided a really important experience for them, one which maybe they will remember and of course I could be really wrong on this!

DAVID: Sounds like a very important experience. I wonder if I can just

COACHING: FACILITATING PERSONAL CHANGE

replay to you some of the words I picked out from what you said that seemed to be important?

David then reads out the list of values and drivers, those things that seemed important to Simon, which he had written down. These included freedom, creativity, energy, inclusiveness, expressiveness, enriching other's experience, teaching, learning.

DAVID: Do these connect with you? Are there words I have missed?

SIMON: No, those are the right ones, yes, that's exactly right. I suppose the only one I'd add is something about there being a bit of a risk, that's important to me. Not too risky but something that takes me a bit out of my comfort zone, that's what gives me energy.

DAVID: Let me add that to the list. Anything else that feels important to you that isn't on this list?

SIMON: There's the play element, there was no performance measurement going on, no targets, just the ability to play with imagination and a story. So playfulness, perhaps. Also I felt I achieved something.

This might go on for a short while, so that the list feels comprehensive.

DAVID: So, it seems as if these are the things that help you feel a sense of fulfilment? I wondered to what extent they are in your life at the moment.

David then brings the focus back to the present and, with Simon, will use these values to inform the goals that emerge in the coaching work.

There are any number of things that can be important to people including recognition, security, being with people or part of a team, giving to others, inclusion by others and thinking things through. By working with a peak experience, as David has done with Simon, the client experiences the feelings associated with the memory, adding to the power of the process. The question: 'What's important to you?' is also valuable as it gives clients an opportunity to list the things that matter. For example, children; the relationship with a partner; being outside; having time to 'be'; creating something; engaging the brain; getting to the 'top' or having enough money.

As therapists we tend to be aware of what clients feel they are missing in their lives and might ask about what really matters to them. Some forms of therapy will work with fulfilment in similar ways to coaching, but often the process attends to the origins or nature of emotional pain rather more than to the client's positive life experiences. As a coach, you will rarely work with the nature or origins of emotional pain, and would most often be working with the positive life experience.

Taking responsibility

The starting point of change is when we are able to take responsibility for the situation we find ourselves in and for what we want instead. When we move from saying: 'I have no choice, I have to do this in this way' to 'I have choices, they have consequences so which choice is going to deliver a better outcome for me?' and when we accept that the only person we can change is us, we are in a position to make changes. Coaching starts from this presumption and encouragement of responsibility.

Therapy also shares this understanding that change needs the acceptance of personal responsibility. Within therapy, real change results once clients are able to take responsibility for their situation. Although in therapy, unlike coaching, the capacity for changing one's circumstances often comes after a long process of working with psycho-emotional disturbances.

Like therapy, coaching separates responsibility and blame. Taking responsibility is not the same as accepting blame. We can accept responsibility for how we have structured our lives and how that is impacting on us now, while also not accepting the blame for those circumstances that led us to create protective and defensive strategies.

Coaching emphasizes this personal responsibility by asking: 'What would you rather have?'; 'If you could change how this affects you, what would you do?'; 'If there were some way in which you were influencing this situation, what might it be?' or 'What might you be able to do differently that might leave you with a different outcome for yourself?'

Coaching clients are introduced to the idea that what they bring to a situation or relationship, in terms of behaviour, beliefs, perceptions, expectations, thoughts and feelings will affect their experience of it and the outcome they get. And, if they change some of those factors, not only will they personally experience it differently, they are also likely to stimulate a different response from other people. This is very familiar territory to therapists, but clients are often not aware of how these dynamics operate.

As coaches, you treat clients consistently as people who can take responsibility for themselves. That is, they are responsible for determining what they want to work on, what goals they wish to achieve and how they decide to go about achieving them. This is modelled throughout a coaching relationship. This is the non-directive aspect of coaching. As soon as you step into giving advice, guidance or directions, you take away some of the clients' responsibility for deciding for themselves and learning from those decisions. While a 'tell and sell' model of ideas giving or direction isn't developmental, it might lead to some short-term actions, but it doesn't allow for learning through deciding, acting and experiencing the consequences. Having said that, it would be irresponsible of any coach to watch a client continue, or set up, a potentially self-damaging process or one which might harm others. If such a situation occurred, the coach should step in, just as a therapist would.

As with therapy, clients will ask you what they should do and for your advice, as the coach, you will need to use skilled ways of avoiding that invitation. For example, Maria was quite anxious in her first coaching session. She wanted Sally, her coach, to tell her what to do and kept asking for guidance and advice. Sally used a number of ways of reflecting the invitation back including:

> Maria, I wonder what you really want for yourself.
>
> Supposing you were giving yourself advice, what would you be telling yourself?
>
> I'm not in a position to advise you what you should do. What we can do though, is explore some of these issues you are bringing and then maybe the way forward will become clearer to you.

Creating wishes and possibilities

As the old saying goes, be careful what you wish for, you might just get it! But without our own wishes, we can all end up living someone else's life. Coaching uses the power of wishes and the capacity to create dreams as a means of visioning a different future, or a future with potential to be satisfying and enlivening. As a coach, your response to clients who say things aren't how they want them to be could be to ask: 'So what would you rather have?' If the answer is: 'I don't know'; you might ask: 'What do you need to do to find out?' or 'Supposing you did know really what you would rather have, what would that be?' The 'I don't know' can be a defence against allowing wishes and dreams to develop. I haven't met anyone yet who didn't really know, but have met several who were too frightened or ashamed to say what they would rather have.

Working with wishes and desires enables clients to create possibilities for themselves, even seemingly 'wild wishes'. For example, 'I'd like to live in the sun and spend my time by the water', can be explored in relation to how feasible that could be, what it would also need to deliver, what might be lost; and can be a turning point in someone's life. Allowing the wish to be spoken, taken seriously and fully explored may result in clients eventually moving to Greece or it may result in their factoring in enough non-working time in the sun, by the sea, to bring a different balance to their life.

Sometimes as a coach you might encourage your clients to generate as many wild wishes as they can, to give full rein to their wish list, to spell out big and small wishes. This is one of my wish lists from a few years ago:

- to be a flamenco dancer
- to live in Spain
- to paint a huge canvas
- to join the country music train in New Mexico
- to be fit, bounce as I walk
- to glow with health
- to open a café and cook some great meals every day
- to grow cabbages.

And to answer your question, no, I haven't achieved all of those wishes but I have achieved some and the others sustain me and I add to them regularly. Wishes generate positive thoughts and hold out the potential of possibility. You will meet clients who find it hard to generate wishes and you may need to enable them to practice.

Sense of agency

By sense of agency or will, I am referring to our capacity to propel ourselves into the future by being able to turn awareness, desire and knowledge into action. It is the bridge between wanting something and taking action to obtain it, and comes when there is a sufficiently integrated sense of self or ego. As a coach, you will be working with clients to engage this sense of agency. A sense of agency or will is not the same as 'will power' which is more about the capacity to override feelings and other needs, to force ourselves to do something. If we want to lose weight, will power is what we need to eat less; our sense of agency is what we use to get our needs met in ways other than with food.

A sense of agency is closely connected to levels of motivation. If people feel highly motivated about something, for example, changing their working practises to give a better work/life balance, they are much more likely to draw on their will to bring it about. If their level of energy for it is low, it won't happen. Low levels of motivation might be affected by beliefs and perceptions which need challenging as they are self-limiting. Low levels of motivation might also be because the goal isn't one which really engages with what the client wants for him or herself or it might be too big a step to take in one stride and needs breaking down. As a coach, you will check out with clients what their levels of commitment and energy are for the goals they set and the actions they propose taking.

CLIENT: I could reshape this work project to enable me to take on more of the research work than I would like.
COACH: I'm not getting a sense of your energy here, on a scale of 0–10, where 10 is you've so much energy you bursting to get on with this and 0 is no energy for it at all, what level does this action hold for you?
CLIENT: Around 6.

Or the coach uses questions like: 'How much energy do you have for this goal (or action) on a scale of 0–10, where 10 is so much energy I can hardly sit still and 0 is absolutely no energy at all?' or 'If your life depended on it, what would you do?' A coach will also check out commitment in the same way. A coaching conversation may go:

SUE (CLIENT): I could apply for that job I talked about, it would give me enough salary, and the work looks interesting.
JAN (COACH): How much energy do you have for doing that on a scale of 0–10?
SUE (after reflecting): About 5.
JAN: Hm, that really doesn't sound like being much energy. What would need to happen to enable you to score it 8 or 9?

A rating of less than 8 or 9 is unlikely to lead to change. As a coach you would continue the work with this client to explore what would be needed for her to feel level 9 energy. That might result in further possibilities and in work with internalized self-limiting beliefs or perceptions. It might result in reframing the goal or possibility as it isn't where the client's real energy is. As a coach, you would test the robustness of commitment as a way also of enabling the client to check out for herself whether this is truly her desired change or if it is something she thinks she could or should do.

A key part of coaching is to enable clients to find out where their motivational energy lies and how it becomes constellated. Without high levels of motivation, personal change cannot happen.

In coaching, you engage this sense of agency by working with goals and by tackling self-limiting beliefs. In this way, you enable clients to bring about the changes they want. People lack the will when the goal isn't theirs; when the perceived benefits don't meet their needs or when they are afraid, for example, of looking stupid, failing or gaining negative responses. Commitment and energy are only engaged when the goal or action fits with our internal values, needs and desires. A lot of work in coaching is in this territory, as once clients have the responsibility plus the will, and have challenged self-limiting beliefs and assumptions, they are ready to make changes in their life.

Will and skills

Coaching works with both will and skill. Both are needed for successful outcomes. It can help to hold this will and skill matrix in mind as a way of thinking about which quadrant represents the client's situation (figure 3.2).

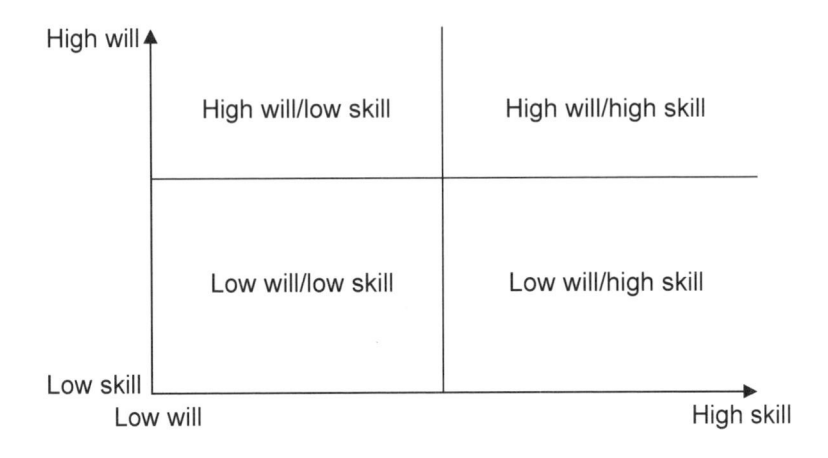

	Low skill	High skill
High will	High will/low skill	High will/high skill
Low will	Low will/low skill	Low will/high skill

Figure 3.2 The will and skill matrix

The coaching process aims to engage the will at high levels of motivation, by connecting the desired outcome with a sense of personal fulfilment. If someone is expressing low will for something, you would focus on what might increase his or her level of motivation. Suppose a client had to do a task that he/she didn't really want to do but it was something required for the job or for family reasons. You might ask: 'How could you make that fun?' or enable him/her to find a way to turn it to provide something he/she wanted. In so doing, you would be helping increase the level of will.

Similarly, those with a highly engaged sense of will or energy to achieve a particular goal or action, but who lack the necessary skills, won't get very far and may lose heart early on. So, as the coach, you would help them explore what skills they might need to achieve what it is they want to achieve, and if they don't know, how they will find out. Their action planning might have to include getting the skills they need, either through accessing training, workshops or self-teaching. This skill development may take some time and the coaching focus might be about keeping the level of motivation high and relating the training to the client's goal. Will alone, therefore, is not always enough; often the hard work is in developing the skills to go along with it.

Karen, a coaching client, who came into coaching to work through a career transformation, decided she really wanted to open a seaside café but had few skills in running such a place. So, she set herself a time scale of when she wanted to achieve that goal, and where, then set out an action plan for how she could best prepare herself by working in other cafés, going on some small business planning workshops, doing some basic food preparation training. She managed these while continuing in her work, fitting them into annual leave and weekends, so that she could also build up some of the financial base she needed. Another client wanted to progress her career by going for a promotion, and identified that she would need to enhance her financial management skills. Encouraged by her coach to explore what, if any, additional skills or experience she might need, she looked at the competences needed for the type of role she wanted to achieve and, using the evidence within her current job, assessed how competent she was. This identified that she needed to increase her knowledge and skills within financial management and she participated in a couple of finance for non-finance manager-type workshops that helped her develop the skills she needed.

Karen had the will to do the work to bring about her aspiration and her coach helped support her to do that. Often clients have aspirations which, when tested against the level of relevant skills they currently have, appear to diminish in feasibility. Testing an ambition, in this way, even when they have a strong will, can confront the client with the reality of what they would have to do to bring it about. Some clients choose to put in the effort; some do not.

Making decisions

Generating and testing wishes and possibilities means that decisions will be needed about which to take forward. As a coach, you will use a range of techniques to enable the client to evaluate options, to test them out, to shape them in the best way possible and to let go of those that fail the test. Personal change, within a coaching model, requires a focused approach so that the energy is directed towards those actions that will deliver the goal sought, and not be wasted on actions that are not goal-focused. People come to decision-making in different ways; some clients rush to make decisions without considering all of the aspects of the decision and others put decisions off, despite considering all aspects. As a coach, you will work with both these positions, and many in between. What matters is for clients to make decisions in their own way, and as the coach, you need to challenge them if they appear to be avoiding moving forward or if their plans seem unrealistic. So, for clients who might appear to rush into a decision, the coach might encourage them to explore whether they have all the information they need and, if not, what else might be useful. They might then test out what could be lost or given up by the decision, or to imagine it is now six months after the decision has been made and invite them to explore in their imagination what the impact of the decision might be. With clients who find it hard to close down a decision, a coach might suggest drawing up some criteria by which to assess the decision. For example, if the client was making a decision about his or her next job, the criteria generated may include the nature of the work, travel distance to work, minimum salary, culture of the organization and perhaps team working. Alternatively the coach might ask a direct challenge: 'How will you know what the best decision is?' Together they might also explore if there are any self-limiting beliefs or thoughts operating that are causing difficulties with decision-making. For example, 'If I do that, I will fail.' It might be that the decision needs some reframing or adjustment as it isn't capturing something that is important for the client.

Taking action and learning

Change requires action and action results in learning. As the coach, you will end all sessions with a direction to action, by asking the following kinds of questions:

> So, Mark, what's the very next step you're going to take to forward this goal before we meet next?
>
> What else are you going to do?
>
> When do you plan to take these actions?
>
> Whose help might you need, and how might you get that?

As a coach, you hold clients to account for the actions they said they would take for themselves. This helps to keep the focus on the change process and the need to take actions, including doing things differently.

Learning is an important part of the coaching process; all action allows for learning. Many of you will be familiar with the learning cycle of action (figure 3.3), that is, having an experience of doing and the response to that from others and within yourself, reflection, theorizing and practical application. All these stages are necessary for learning to occur.

Many of us spend most of our time in the action part of the cycle, that is acting and responding, acting and responding. Through coaching, clients are

```
            Action
              ▲
             ╱ ╲
            ╱   ╲
           ╱     ╲
          ╱       ▼
    Planning    Reflection
          ▲       ╱
           ╲     ╱
            ╲   ╱
             ╲ ▼
         Generalization
```

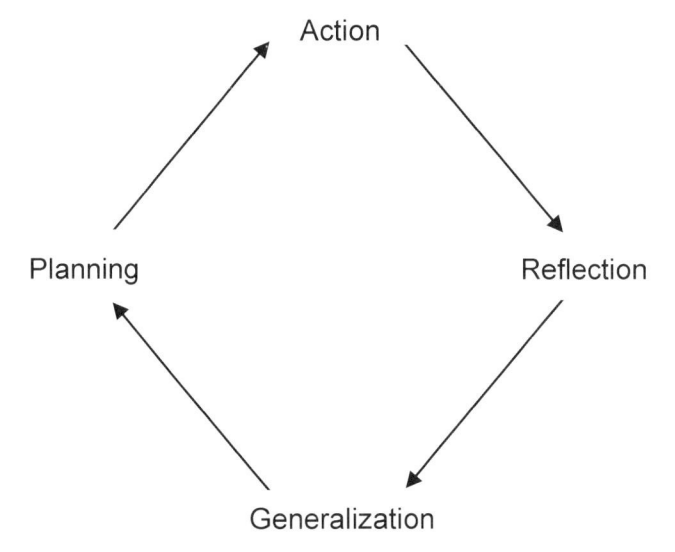

Figure 3.3 The learning cycle of action

encouraged to identify what they have learnt by reflecting on questions like: 'Of all the things you did, which do you think had the most impact?'; 'Knowing what you now know, what might you have done differently?' or 'When you do something like this again, what might you do differently?' With all learning, it is important not to get into judgements of failure, success, good or bad as they all limit the extent of learning. We can just get hung up on what we did that was wrong.

Coaching uses the concept of Appreciative Inquiry, based on David Cooperrider's work at Case Western University (Cooperrider and Whitney 2005). This is a solutions-focused, positive psychology approach, that highlights what went well with the idea that if we know what behaviour or action works we should do more of it. In this way it differs from a problem-focused approach of finding out what didn't work, and trying not to do it again. Using this approach, coaching questions might include: 'What were the skills that you took to that situation which had the most impact?' or 'What was special about how you approached that situation which, if we could capture it, you could use in other situations?' It takes some practice to avoid using the word *good*, which inevitably carries a judgement with it. Coaching is a personal development process, that includes the enhancement of self-awareness and the capacity to learn and to build on that learning.

Clients for whom coaching might not be the best option

As a coach, you might come across clients who aren't able to take up the challenge of personal change. This may be because of trauma or developmental disturbance that has resulted in a fragmented sense of self or other psycho-emotional disturbance. In such instances, the individual is more likely to be helped by psychological therapy. People who want help with troubling internal emotional disturbances, for example, who are suffering:

- Intense grief
- Overwhelmong feelings, such as depression
- Symptoms of internal disturbance, such as an eating disorder or obsessive behaviour
- Intense anxiety states

All are better helped by therapy. They are less likely to be able to take up a position of agency, which is needed for the coaching process, as that needs a sufficiently integrated sense of self. As a therapist, you are more likely to be able to identify where this might be the case and unfortunately, also more likely to see the potential need for therapy in everyone. A non-therapeutically trained coach may need training to be able to identify those clients who might be better helped by therapy.

Most clients choose appropriately. If they need therapy, they tend to contact a therapist. If they feel able to take on coaching and it fits with what they want to achieve through the process, they are likely to contact a coach. They know what they need. If however, a client, whom we will call Sarah, came to talk to you about coaching and you had a sense that perhaps that wasn't the best route for her, you would explore with her what led her to choose coaching and whether she had considered other ways of working, including therapy. That might lead to an exploration of any self-limiting beliefs about therapy or it might demonstrate she had made a clear choice to come to coaching and felt able to work in that way. Alternatively it might lead to a discussion about the coaching process in terms of what it does and doesn't involve. This might result in her confirming coaching as a choice over therapy, or vice versa. Clients who are unable to use coaching tend not to stay in the process for long.

Sometimes clients come to coaching wanting something different but perhaps not knowing how to access it or not feeling it would be OK to go into a therapy relationship. Taking a coaching approach can help them work this through for themselves. The coach doesn't need to tell or advise them what to do.

Pam came to a coach as she felt stuck and unable to find which direction to take, having just ended a successful period of her life. A friend had suggested that maybe coaching would be useful. In the first session, the coach, John, felt some resistance from Pam to engage with things about the future or to engage with the process. He wasn't sure what to make of this but had a sense that there was something going on internally that was not being articulated in the first session. John felt there was something unresolved regarding her relationship with her father but had no real hard evidence for that; it was a hunch. He prepared for the second session and wasn't surprised when Pam came and said that she hadn't really taken anything forward from the first session. That fitted with his hunch. He invited Pam to say what she wanted from this session; she said she wasn't sure and wasn't sure if coaching was going to be helpful to her. He asked her if she had had any thoughts about what she felt might be more helpful. That led to Pam to talk about thinking about going to psychotherapy, with a lot of hesitations. The outcome was that John coached Pam around what she wanted from psychotherapy, how she might find the right person to work with and in what time scale. When he checked out motivation with her, he wasn't surprised to find a higher level of energy for that process.

4 Coaching framework

Coaching is a holistic process; it accommodates all aspects of the client's life and the balance between them. People often come into coaching when their lives have got out of balance. For example, over-focusing on work may have pushed out meeting their need for spiritual development or their need for exercise or leisure. Working with the totality of clients' lives enables them to reflect on the interrelationship between the various aspects, to work through how changes in one may affect satisfaction in the others. What is important is that clients identify what a good balance for them would be and identify where they want to place the focus within the coaching (figure 4.1).

Professional and working life

- Personal ambitions
- Nature of work/career
- Personal effectiveness
- Work/home environment/location
- **Inner Processes**
- Money
- Health, leisure and well-being
- Personal relationships, including friends, family, special other
- Spiritual/soul & artistic life
- Personal growth

Personal life

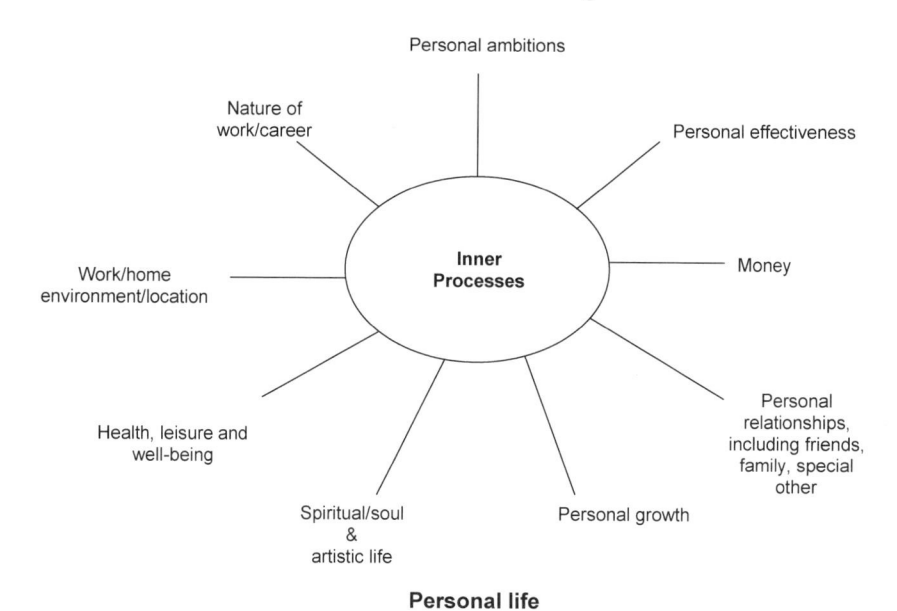

Figure 4.1 Balance between professional and personal life

The components of the holistic frame cover the client's professional, personal and relational life:

- *Personal ambitions*: what you want for yourself, how satisfied you are with the extent to which your ambitions have been or are being realized.
- *Personal effectiveness*: how satisfied you are with your level of skills, and your ability to use those skills in different situations.
- *Money*: how satisfied or concerned you are with your financial situation; the extent to which money is important to you.
- *Personal relationships, including friends, family and a special other*: how satisfying are these relationships? Are there things that aren't going the way you'd like? How important are they to you?
- *Personal growth*: how satisfied are you with your personal development? Is your personal development enabling you to grow in the ways you want?
- *Spiritual/soul and artistic life*: how satisfying is this part of your life? Are you doing the amount of 'soul work' or artistic/creative expression that is important or necessary for you? Perhaps your faith is important to you, are you expressing that in the way you want? Is your life providing the meaning you seek?
- *Health, leisure and well-being*: do you feel healthy and as fit as you would like to? Is there something about your health that needs addressing? Perhaps you have noticed changes in your sleeping or eating patterns, or levels of physical energy? What about leisure activities? Are they providing you with what you need?
- *Work/home environment or location*: do your home and work-space and surroundings provide what you need for your own health and well-being? What about your travel to work, time or process, is that working sufficiently for you?
- *Nature of work/career*: how satisfying is your work and career to you just now? Is your work fulfilling? To what extent is your career moving forward in the way you hoped?

Take a moment to reflect for yourself the level of your satisfaction in each of these, using a rating of 0–10, where 10 is totally satisfied. What do you notice as you do this?

Most coaches take their clients through a similar kind of reflective process, to map the whole picture, to raise issues and look at the interrelationships. As the coach, it is important that you hold an holistic approach and framework when working with your clients. What is sufficient or acceptable in each area is the clients' judgement and clients will vary greatly. What you might notice is that their satisfaction is focused in a few areas or there are low levels of satisfaction across all parts of life. You might also find that some clients settle for low levels of satisfaction sometimes from the belief that that is all they should expect for themselves. Some levels of dissatisfaction may be temporary. For example, if the client has building work going on at home or work, then he or she is likely to rate his/her level of satisfaction with home/work environment as low. There may, however, be some short-term coping strategies that it might be useful for clients to explore, if that is where they want their focus to be. In the spirit of 'the client is responsible', it is up to clients to identify which areas they most want to work on.

Coaching has a clear framework of principles that define the process and orientation to the work, and to some extent, differentiates it from other processes.

Orientation of the coach

One of the ways to ensure clients are protected is for coaches to adhere to a set of core coaching principles and a code of practice. These include a commitment to confidentiality, respect and empathy for clients and a commitment to valuing and working with difference and diversity. Clients need to be able to trust the integrity and honesty of the coach. As the coach, you demonstrate this trustworthiness through your ethical behaviour and by adhering to the principles of coaching. These will be very familiar to psychological therapists and will, hopefully, already underpin your work with clients.

Clients know what they need

Even though clients may not always believe this, as the coach you need to believe it. As the coach, you are providing a confidential and explorative space for clients to enable them to play with ideas and wishes, to be able to voice those and to know that they won't be ridiculed or dismissed but taken seriously. The difference between wants and needs is always a difficult area, but clients know if what they say they want isn't really what they need, they are able to hold the two together. As the coach, you will be reality-testing and grounding ideas with them that will help with this process.

Jane, a client, was in the middle of a difficult career transition; she was facing redundancy and thinking of alternative things she would like to do. One of the ideas that energized her was to open a dress shop; she could imagine herself doing that and enjoying it. With her coach she explored the skills she would need and reality-tested things like money, premises and staffing. In doing that, she realized her plans were not achievable, but rather than just drop it, her coach invited her to reflect on what it was about opening a dress shop that really engaged her. Out of that came things like: being more of my own boss, meeting people, helping them choose a special outfit, having a different relationship with people at work. Jane then added these to other things that were important to her to look at how she could get some of them in a different, more feasible way. She knew what she needed but her idea for meeting those needs did not quite fit.

Clients know if they need emotional or therapeutic work; they haven't stumbled into coaching by mistake but have made a choice. I have had clients who have shared information about childhood trauma, including sexual abuse and bullying, and who have articulated the connections they see from that experience, and their response to it, to issues within their current situation. There have been times when I have wondered whether they would be helped by counselling or therapy. But remembering that the client is responsible, I have raised that with them and each time they have said something like: 'No, I don't feel that is what I need to do now. I know what it is about, there may be a time later when I feel I need to do something more about it but for now I just wanted you to know but I don't want to do any more with it.'

Clients know what they need. If we don't believe that, we are in effect saying: 'We know what they need', but how can we? It can be difficult, at times, for therapists to accept this, as we may identify psychological and emotional factors that we believe need resolving for the client to achieve his or her full potential. As coaching isn't a process of looking inwards and downwards into the 'underworld' of our psycho-emotional lives, it may not appeal to therapists who believe that the only way to achieve personal change is to work in that way. Such therapists are likely to consider that the client's desire not to go inwards and downwards is a defence or escape from engaging at a deeper, psycho-emotional or psycho-social level. This is a valid view and this approach may be relevant to some clients at certain times. However, it also suggests that coaching is a superficial process. This is not my experience or such therapists may believe that coaching doesn't work with important internalized structures. Again, this is not the case. Coaching can be a life-changing and deeply meaningful process for clients.

The client is resourceful

The coach has to have the belief that clients are fully resourceful; that is, they have all the inner resources of imagination, energy, focus and drive they need to propel themselves forward and to achieve the outcomes they seek. The client is not seen as lacking in capability or deficient in any way. A good start is for coaches to believe that they too are fully resourceful, that they have all the resources that the client needs from them. This does not mean, however, that the client may not identify the need to develop new skills, knowledge or abilities, or to create resources (such as time, money or help from others). Nor does it mean you, the coach, have all the skills, knowledge, abilities or external resources you may need to be effective. What it does mean is that, given the right environment, you can access inner resourcefulness to determine the path you want to follow, and set about travelling that path to the outcome. That travelling may involve skills development, relationship building, networking, knowledge acquisition, changing habits, challenging internal sabotage, experimentation with different activities, any number of things all focused on achieving the desired goal.

Coaching is future-focused

Coaching looks forward not backwards; it emphasizes goals and actions. It uses questions like: 'What would you rather have?' rather than: 'How did things get to be like this?' As the coach, your aim is to hold the future-focus, to help the client to move forwards. You will also be holding a solutions-focused orientation, working with the client to find solutions, not to define or redefine the problem (table 4.1).

Table 4.1 Comparison of past-focused thinking and future-focused thinking

Past-focused thinking	Future-focused thinking
What's wrong?	What would be better?
Whose fault?	Self-responsibility
Problems	Possibilities
Defining and explaining	Actions
Negative thinking	Positive thinking
Deficits	Resourcefulness
Why?	What next?

The starting point in coaching is *now*. From the *now* clients are encouraged to identify the goals they want to achieve and that are meaningful to them. Goals help hold the movement 'towards the future' and are the corner-stone of coaching. Without them, coaching flounders and no change results. The future might be two or three years ahead or next month. There is no prescription about the distance into the future other than sufficiently far enough ahead to draw clients forward. For example, Mark wants to change the direction of his career and find a way of moving out of the city and working for himself. He has set himself the time frame of achieving this within the next 18 months. John wants to reconfigure his job and is aiming in doing that within three or four months. Susan has a goal she wants to achieve within two weeks and is going to focus her time to do that.

Goal-setting is rather like putting an anchor into the future; the anchor chain provides a connection to the future and the client can pull themselves along it as they move forward. The future is a concept, given that all we really have is the *now*, so being future-focused is a way of enabling our *nows* to fit better our values and needs.

In this aspect, coaching is different from many forms of therapy in that it does not particularly attend to the causal factors within the clients' history; it is not concerned with the *why*, the reason a client is like they are or why they are in the situation they are in. The emphasis is on visualizing and then creating a different experience from now on.

In coaching, the past, or internalized experience, is only relevant to the extent to which there is something to be learned or affirmed from it. For example, as a coach you might find yourself asking: 'Was there a time in your life when you felt things were going just the way you wanted, when you felt you were really living to your values?'; 'Have you found yourself in similar situations in the past? If so, what helped you most to move on?' or 'What resources did you draw on that helped you most in the past?' In these questions the emphasis is on learning from the past, it is also on what worked and not on what went wrong. Coaching keeps solutions focused.

As a coach, you will rarely explore biography or developmental history. That isn't to say you never will, as knowing something about clients' life events is important. For example, as part of the initial session you may ask the client to tell you about his or her life and significant life events. This will give you some sense of what has had an impact on the client's life and what his or her responses have been.

Coaching is an adult:adult relationship

Using the transactional analysis (TA) concept of ego-states helps us describe the coaching relationship. In fact, TA, a humanistic orientation, has many principles which are similar to coaching. For example, Ian Stewart, in his book *TA Today* (1987), talks of the philosophical assumptions of TA being that people are OK; everyone has the capacity to think and people decide their own destiny, and these decisions can be changed.

You may be familiar with the TA concept of parent, adult and child ego-states that we all carry within us and which are expressed through a range of different behaviour patterns (Eric Berne, *Games People Play*, 1964). From the parent ego-state we replay behaviour, feelings and thought patterns that we learnt from parent figures in the past. These include aspects of control and boundary setting as well as caring, nurturing and protective behaviour.

The child ego-state carries behaviour, feelings and thought patterns that we experienced in our past, in response to those around us, and continue to carry with us. These include behaviour associated with fitting in or complying with others, preventing us being our real selves, as well as that behaviour concerned with revealing feelings, needs, acting on impulse, being energetic, excited and creative.

The adult ego-state is associated with the here and now, processing information rationally, developing possibilities, using experience and learning from it, identifying probabilities and decision-making. That is, without the transference or projections from the parent or child ego-states.

This is, of course, a very simple description of a more complex set of ideas, however, even in its simplicity, it can help describe the nature of the coaching relationship.

Coaching is based on securing an adult:adult relationship. That is, the coach aims to work primarily from the adult ego-state and, in so doing, to bring clients into working from their adult ego-state, from which they can make decisions, engage their will to act in the world, take responsibility and action. The adult ego-state is more associated with thinking than feeling, and, therefore, as the coach, you need to have full access to the positive aspects of the other ego-states within yourself and to help your clients similarly achieve that.

Coaching also draws on the energy and creativity associated with the natural or free child, bringing a sense of playfulness in to allow new possibilities and ideas to arise. As a coach, you might use a phrase such as: 'Let's just play with this for a moment', in order to help clients access their natural child ego-state and to silence their internal critical parent (or negative superego, depending on your orientation). Playfulness is an important aspect of coaching; the ability to let go of the internalized rules about what should or must happen, about having to succeed, be perfect or work hard. Playing with ideas and using the imagination enables us also to explore the possible behaviour, feelings and thoughts that might go with a different type of experience. We can give ourselves a different experience within our imagination.

As the coach, you will also speak from your parent ego-state at times. For example, setting out the contract is about control to some extent although it is negotiated with clients so that they are making an adult decision and choice. You will also have a need at times to speak from the nurturing and caring parent ego-state, to offer the client support; not to do so could leave you being detached, impersonal or experienced as being rather cold. As coaches, therapists and counsellors, you have to be careful that you are not responding inappropriately or without being aware of what you are doing. You may, for example, smother clients with your protectiveness or demand that they do what you think they should. Ensuring that you operate from a sense that clients are responsible for themselves will help to avoid the potentially negative aspects of these ego-states.

The coach is proactive and non-directive

As a coach, you are actively engaged in the coaching process. This proactive stance is reflected in the depth of your listening and in the nature of your interventions. You are 'on the front foot' ready to offer something of relevance and usefulness to clients; you are not sitting back, leaving them to do the work alone.

All coaches have a tool kit of exercises and techniques that are used to enable clients to explore a situation, to engage their imaginations and to reframe their perceptions and beliefs. As the coach, you are therefore actively listening for understanding and to be able to take up a position of empathy with clients. At the same time you are listening for what the coaching edge might be, what might be a useful next step within this session. As a coach, you need to be able to do both, simultaneously. The appropriateness of an exercise, process or the nature of the intervention is entirely dependent on the quality of the listening the coach has been engaged in.

Coaching is non-directive. To that effect, I have already talked about resisting the temptation to advise or give guidance. However, coaching is also non-directive to the extent that the coach only suggests a particular exercise and genuinely gives clients permission not to go in that direction if it doesn't feel right for them. If you are in an adult:adult relationship, this is likely to be the case; if you have slipped into a parent:child relationship, the client may feel obliged to do as you suggest or to resist your suggestions at all costs. If clients pick up on the coach's ideas or suggestions as a matter of course, the coach will check for motivational energy and commitment and might challenge clients about taking responsibility for generating their own ideas.

Similarly, as a coach, you may have some ideas that you think might be useful to the client's situation. There are many ways in which these ideas can be put into the process, along with the ideas generated by the client. If the client isn't interested in them, or other suggestions, you must let them go. This non-directiveness is embedded in the process, even if you think a particular exercise might be useful, the decision as to whether to follow that suggestion has to be the client's.

Transition *and* transformation

Coaching is about transition *and* transformation. Some clients may come to coaching to be helped through a transition, to manage a job change or relocation or handle a period of change. Other clients are looking for, or come to desire, some more fundamental transformation. For example, a radical change perhaps in their career direction, to how they live their lives or to how they think about themselves. As a coach, you will offer opportunities for transformation to all clients. These may be in relation to the transformation of thoughts, beliefs or in relation to major life changes.

The use of creativity and imagination is vital in enabling old patterns, or habits of thinking to be broken. Transformation cannot be achieved without engaging internalized energy and without much work to liberate beliefs, assumptions and perceptions. Transformation also requires the capacity to take what might feel like a considerable risk. In these situations, coaching can help hold and reduce the sense of the size of the risk; it can therefore make all the difference to clients' abilities to make changes. Some clients are more creative than others, and how clients use their imagination varies. As the coach, you need to be skilled at working with differing levels and forms of creativity and imagination.

Working with feelings

Clients can experience deep feelings in the coaching process and boxes of tissues are as much a feature of the coaching room as they are the therapy room. Coaching doesn't use emotional processing as part of the change process. It works with feelings in a different way. In coaching, you are working with the clients' thoughts (beliefs, perceptions, assumptions) and the feelings that are associated with those thoughts. As you work with clients to reframe their thoughts, you will ask them what feelings are associated with the new thoughts. You will ask: 'How does that feel?' when testing out a new thought or idea, or when reflecting on an exercise. You will also challenge clients to consider: 'If you were able to do X without feeling frightened, is it something you would want?' In so doing, you are seeking to separate the feelings from thoughts and to set up a different association with the client. A coaching client may say: 'I want to feel happy.' A coaching response might be: 'If you felt happy, what would you be doing differently?' It would not seek to explore the felt experience in more depth nor to define the source of the unhappiness. If a client says: 'I feel so unhappy', you, as a coach, would be empathetic to that state and then enquire: 'What would you rather feel?' You would not encourage the client to stay with the negative feelings. Coaching is less focused on the affect or emotional state of clients than many therapeutic processes.

Jessica is a coaching client in her thirties. During one session she talks about her father who is chronically ill at the other end of the country. She talks about her father and becomes emotional, sad and tearful, as she contemplates his impending death. Peter, the coach, provides an empathic response giving space for the affect. At the 'right time', which he judged to be when the full force of her tearfulness was easing, he made a directive suggestion.

PETER: I can see how this is affecting you. I wonder what actions, if any, you may want to take if you could do whatever you wanted.

In broaching this he left her the option not to pick up on actions and to stay with the feeling experience if that is what she wanted. For example, she might say: 'No, there's nothing I want to do differently, it just feels good to acknowledge the impact it is having on me.' Peter is also shifting from emotional processing to a coaching approach that is solutions-focused and cognitive-behavioural. He might also have asked her the following question:

PETER: I can see how this is affecting you. I wonder whose support you need right now?

By that he is prompting her to think about what support she needs for this emotional time.

Jessica's response to his first question about what actions, if any, might be:

JESSICA: What I really want to do is go there right now just to reassure myself that he is getting the help he needs.

PETER: What would you need to do, to do that?

Jessica responds with all of the reasons why she can't, because of work and other commitments. Peter works with this and Jessica realizes to herself that going this week would be difficult but she could go the next week if she wanted to. Peter might also have said to her:

PETER: What is likely to happen if you don't go, or if there were ways of reassuring yourself that didn't involve going today, what might they be?

In this way, he is inviting her to think of other possibilities and to explore the totality of the *now* situation. He is working with her about what next, he isn't taking her back into the history of the relationship with her father or encouraging her to remain with the pain of his impending death. Nor is he ignoring these feelings or being insensitive to them.

A different example of how coaching works with feelings involves James and his coach working with a self-limiting belief. The coach, Martin, has asked James to write up the opposite of his self-limiting belief which was about being successful.

MARTIN: How does it feel when you hear yourself say this reframed belief, that it is OK to enjoy your success?

James becomes emotional and realizes that the negative self-belief had some links with his father and brother, thus providing new insights for him. Had Martin been in therapy mode, it might be very tempting to follow James down the historical and emotional route. However, Martin stayed in coaching mode and gave James space to talk about this new insight and then returned to the work on the self-limiting belief.

Martin:	These sound like important insights. I'm wondering whether it feels possible to believe that you can be successful and enjoy that success.
James:	Yes, it does. I am aware of how things make me believe that it isn't possible, but I do think I can believe the opposite.

In this way the coach has used feelings to explore the response to a reframed belief and in so doing, produced some valuable insights. The coach hasn't stayed in an emotional processing mode but has given sufficient space for the affect. The coach might also have asked: 'Is there anything about your relationship with your father or brother that you would like to change?' That would move James into thinking about goals and actions.

Content-free space for exploration

Coaching is content-free. That is, a skilled coach could provide effective coaching to anyone regardless of the context within which clients live or work. As a coach, you are providing clients with an environment and frame, within which there can be confidential, safe, inspirational and collegiate space for day dreaming, visioning a different future, exploring and testing possibilities without judgements or limitations imposed by others or by their own internalized limitations. The coach's function is to bring to the relationship skills, tools and techniques that meet clients' needs and agenda. In this way space for transformation is provided.

5 Differences between therapy and coaching

While there are many similarities between therapy and coaching, there are also differences. When training therapists to become coaches, there are several questions often asked as people come to an understanding of what those similarities and differences are in relation to their therapeutic orientation and practice.

Coaching is not about healing

Coaching is not another way of doing therapy. I know I have stated this a number of times, but it is an important factor to bear in mind. Coaching doesn't use a metaphor of healing and the client isn't seen as wounded, damaged, in pain or as needing a restorative process. Clients should not be encouraged to consider themselves in this way either. As the coach, you are not taking up a healing or nursing function. You don't need to 'take care' of clients or protect them. You do need to be caring and compassionate, but you don't need to think for them. The clients are seen as healthy, having all the resources they need and as being capable of moving themselves forward into the future. While as a coach, you are to some extent in a helping relationship with the client, it is primarily about working together, not being a 'helper' assisting someone who is disabled or ill. Together you are curious about what the future could hold for the clients, how they can engage more of themselves with the life they lead or how they can be even more effective within their chosen goals and ambitions. There is a spirit of adventure.

Diagnosis-free

Like other humanistic orientations, coaching is diagnosis-free. It doesn't follow a medical model and there are no diagnostic categories or analysis needed by the coach in relation to clients' psycho-emotional experience. The only diagnosis is done by clients, in terms of where they want the emphasis of their work to be, together with the associations they may make to their developmental or social history.

Free association

Coaching doesn't use a free association methodology, that is, where clients relate what is in their mind or inner experience and the therapist listens for connections and clues to the unconscious or other processes. Coaching is a focused process where clients are asked what they want to work on and what they want to get from the session. The work is then closely aligned to those goals. If clients deviate into storytelling or conversational mode, as the coach you will interrupt them and ask whether what they were talking about was what they want to be working on.

Working with the unconscious processes

Many therapies use free association as a way of illuminating unconscious processes, for example, projections and defence systems. Coaching doesn't work with the unconscious in this way; it doesn't use interpretation as part of its methodology. Nor does coaching aim to provoke unconscious material.

As a coach, however, you will need to be aware of your own responses to clients, those which maybe they have stimulated in you by their projections, and those that come from your own internal material. This awareness is a valuable resource. You might, for example, become aware of being pushed into, or taking up, a parental role and use that insight to bring the relationship back into adult:adult through the nature of your questioning. You would not use it to interpret to the client what you thought was happening.

You might also become aware that clients are provoking some reaction within you; you are then able to prevent yourself acting on that stimulus inappropriately. For example, without this awareness you might push them in one direction or another unconsciously, or fail to encourage them in some way. It is for this reason that coaches need supervision just the same as therapists and counsellors, to protect client and the coach. The question all coaches need to hold onto is: 'Is this the client's agenda or mine?' Whenever it becomes the coach's agenda, the process is being compromised.

Catharsis and re-experiencing

Since coaching is not focused on the assimilation of experience, it does not use catharsis or re-experiencing to reconnect with developmental events. Coaching doesn't go backwards; its aim is to move forwards.

For example, if a coaching client, Mary, wants to be better able to speak with confidence at conferences to further her goal of professional achievement, she may describe the memory of an incident when she felt her public speaking was a disaster. A coaching response may be to do some affirmation work around that experience by exploring: 'While you remember it this way, I wondered what small things, perhaps, looking back you *can* be pleased about' plus: 'This feels like it is becoming a self-limiting memory, how could we shift it into an incident from which you could learn?'

The coach may also suggest to Mary that she do a guided imagery exercise based on a memory when she was pleased with her speaking performance. The coaching approach is to replace the negative thoughts and feelings associated with the event with positive ones and to balance them with other more affirmative and forward moving thoughts. As coach, you would not encourage Mary to engage with the feeling experience of shame or its possible origins by exploring with her any associations or memories she may have.

Method or the person?

Coaching operates within a relationship, therefore, the person who is the coach is a factor. If the client likes the coach, feels understood and 'met', a rapport is established which will have a strong influence on the work and the extent to which the client is able to use the coaching. However, coaching is a methodology with tools and techniques that have been shown to work repeatedly with different clients in different contexts. It is the coach's ability to select and use the suited methods, tools and techniques in an appropriate and timely way, together with the integrity of the coach that makes the most difference within coaching. Having said that, a relationship with trust, respect, acceptance and encouragement has to be present for coaching to be effective. It is just that the work isn't embedded in the relationship; clients aren't learning about themselves through how they respond to or impact on the coach in the same way they do in some therapies.

Many people go through life never feeling encouraged to explore their wishes and desires, or receiving positive responses to their ideas. The coach is encouraging and positive, while also enabling clients to test ideas against reality and motivation. The experience of being encouraged can be one of the most powerful elements of the coaching process. It gives clients permission to dream and to allow them to think through what they really want for themselves, not what others need them to do or expect them to do. Encouragement can, therefore, provide a challenge to clients' internalized parent ego-state or negative super-ego by offering a different experience and enabling the client to shift from an either/or position. This encouragement doesn't come from the coach's parent ego-state. In the encouragement, you are not recreating or creating a parent:child dynamic. You are speaking as a trusted colleague or peer.

Speed of change

Coaching can bring about change in a short time frame. In coaching, change can happen as a result of each session. It doesn't happen at the end of a process it *is* the process. Clients who are able to call on a sense of agency, with a sufficiently integrated sense of self, are able to bring about changes throughout a coaching process. Moreover, the process is designed to bring that about. The aim of coaching is that clients will make personal changes in those areas of their life that they have chosen to change.

My understanding is that in the early days of psychoanalysis, analyses were in fact relatively short, around three months. It has become a longer process, it is suggested, because we know more and have a richer body of theory on which to draw. There is also some suggestion, as yet unproven by research, that change is produced more quickly when people have no vocabulary in psychoanalysis or therapy, no internalized language with which to explain or justify their situation. I am not sure how robust the evidence is on this but it is an interesting thought. Coaching doesn't use the language of psychoanalysis or therapy and doesn't encourage clients to describe themselves in psychological terms. It could be that this also helps the speed of change. The language of coaching is uncomplicated; the questions and interventions are succinct and specific. The coach isn't putting together ideas or formulations that might, at times, appear complex to a client.

Coaching can quickly move someone out of an either/or mode of thinking and allow other possibilities to emerge which can be put into action. This either/or frame can be immobilizing: 'Either I have to work all hours to pay the bills or I will be destitute' or 'Either I have to put up with their responses to me or I will be on my own.' As neither option is attractive, clients choose the one that appears to protect them the most. The result is low motivation, low energy and a sense of being trapped. This either/or way of thinking is familiar to many therapists; clients will often talk about their options in this way and as a therapist, you might explore why they see things in that way. A coaching response is to explore: 'If there were sets of options in-between those points, what might they be?' or, as the coach, you would offer an exercise that will enable the client to create a vision of a possible alternative, one that releases some energy and enables the client to move forward.

Coaching confronts the internal resistances to change. It uses a range of techniques for challenging and changing self-limiting beliefs or memories, and that inner voice that tells us we are stupid, will fail, will never make anything of ourselves or don't deserve any different. As a coach, you will be skilled at working with this resistance and will work with the client to dismiss or replace these beliefs and to develop techniques for dealing with the inner voice of negativity. It is this aspect of coaching which is also crucial to producing change.

Some psychological therapists may be attracted to coaching because it offers this opportunity for change to happen more quickly. It can be frustrating and exhausting working with clients who are struggling with relational and life defences. In many therapies, the right thing is for the therapist to be able to bear this frustration so that clients are able to find their way in their own time through a deep and difficult internal process. Coaching can also be frustrating and coaches, like therapists, can find themselves wondering: 'Why won't the client do what they clearly want/need to do? Why is this taking so long?' Clients suffer setbacks by getting caught up in self-limiting beliefs or by sabotaging their own efforts, and change can at times be one step forward and two steps back. All your skills as a therapist, in staying with the clients' process and your commitment to the work, will be valuable to you as a coach.

All of us, coaches and therapists alike, can allow our needs or anxieties to be uppermost. For example, our need for the client to change or get well, so that we get feedback that we are doing a good job. In coaching, some clients make changes swiftly with a lot of motivation, others take longer. They stumble and keep erecting defences against change. As a coach, you need to be able to keep with the work, maintain the focus, repeatedly challenging the self-limiting beliefs and using them to learn from the process.

Shame

Many people feel shame at asking for help or for being needy. This can prevent people from accessing psychotherapy and counselling, as that can be shameful. Counselling and psychotherapy can carry associations with mental ill health, which similarly carries shame in our society. Interestingly, people who self-refer to coaching don't appear to experience that shame in accessing coaching; in those situations, coaching doesn't carry a stigma of neediness or mental illness but is seen as being a positive thing, like going to the gym. This is not always the case with clients who have been required to participate in coaching by their organization or who work in a setting where coaching and personal development aren't the norm. Their fear is that if people found out, they would think the client was struggling with the job, and that would be shameful. As a coach, therefore, you have to be as sensitive as you would be with a therapy client, to the potential for shame in relation to the relationship.

Shame arises in coaching when you are working with clients on their self-limiting beliefs. These can often be based on avoiding shameful situations, for example, failing, and it can be shameful to talk about aspects of our negative self.

Does shame contribute to people wanting to work short-term, or gain quick results, because it would be shameful to need to work for a long time or to be unable to turn things around? This is, of course, a factor and the coach needs to be aware of this and to challenge such perceptions or beliefs so as to enable clients to replace them with differently affirming thoughts. Some clients may access coaching to avoid the shame of needing deeper, longer-term work within a therapeutic frame. However, if the coach is doing their job properly, this will emerge in the work and clients will be enabled to take up the help they feel they need, and to leave coaching.

Spiritual dimension

Coaching includes spiritual needs, whether they are based on faith, creativity or a higher self; that part of us that seeks fulfilment and provides us with meaning to our lives. Some people differentiate between psychotherapy and coaching saying the former is about the soul, using a definition of therapy as 'liberating resources of the soul and spirit or that which is beyond the constructs of personality or psycho-social defences'. Coaching can also be about liberating these resources. It might go about it in a different way but if that is what clients are seeking, coaching will help take them there. I worked with a client, Rob, a few years ago who was a very successful person according to the criteria of financial and career achievements, also in his relationships. However, an organizational merger offered him an opportunity to take stock and think about what he really wanted for himself. He decided he wanted to go on a spiritual journey, to let go and follow his instinct. We worked on how he could set this up and then we ended the coaching. Three years later, I got a letter telling me what had happened. Rob had got rid of a lot of his possessions, had bought a small camper van and set off. He painted, did some writing, looked at the sea, went on a range of different types of workshops, participated in a Buddhist retreat and met a lot of interesting people. He did soul work. He came to that through coaching. He might well have got there on his own but coaching provided a vehicle for it becoming a reality and not 'something I'll do when I find a space in my life'.

Another client felt very pressurized at work and we looked at all of the things that were going on and how she might structure things differently. We then talked about where she got her creativity fuel from, what nurtured her and kept her soul alive. It transpired that over the years her artistic self had gone into a coma, for all sorts of reasons, and she was no longer going to art galleries, having artistic treats, writing short stories, painting, things that kept her alive internally. This lack of creative fuel was affecting her working energy and creativity. So we looked together at how she might bring these inner resources back into her life, how she wanted them to be part of her life in the future. The presenting issues were work related but alongside those were these issues about resources of the spiritual self.

Meaningfulness

I have had many conversations in which some therapists/counsellors have dismissed coaching as being light-weight and superficial, and others where coaches have dismissed psychotherapy/counselling as being long-winded and bringing an unnecessary focus on pain and distress. Neither of these are true. Coaching can be experienced as a deep, penetrating and life changing experience through which clients create a closer attunement between what they need for themselves to feel enriched and for life to have meaning, and their actual life experience. At times, we need therapy and counselling processes to be with our innermost selves, giving space to personal growth, to bring about often complex internal resolutions and develop a deeper self-awareness.

There are many roads that can take us towards the same place. Some might be more twisted and be steeper, some scenic, while others traverse more barren landscapes. Each teaches us something different, and through each we get in touch with different resources and responses. Coaching can provide one of these roads. Therapy (in all its forms), group analysis and meditation (and other more spiritual journeys) offer different routes at different times of life and for different people and purposes. Each road can be difficult and challenging and each can be deeply meaningful.

52 THERAPIST INTO COACH

Reflective exercise

This might be a good point to reflect on the similarities and differences you have noticed, so far, between coaching and your orientation and practice as a therapist.

Table 5.1 Comparison between coaching and therapy

Aspect of coaching	*Similar or different? If different, in what way?*
Integration of *cognitive-behavioural* and *humanistic/person-centred* orientations	
Application of *motivational theories*	
Approach to achieving personal change: Clients are responsible; giving space for wishes; engaging with sense of agency (motivation and will); decision-making; action and learning	
Orientation of the coach: Trustworthy, offering confidentiality; ethical practice; honest; valuing diversity and difference; committed to the client relationship	
Coaching framework: Clients know what they want and need; clients have all the resources they need; future-focus consistently held; focused on goals and action; adult:adult relationship; coach is proactive and non-directive	

6 The coaching relationship

Establishing a coaching relationship has much in common with how you create a therapy relationship. As a coach, you will use all your skills in rapport building and establishing contact with the client; meeting the client from an orientation of empathy and positive regard. The nature of the relationship is that of equal co-workers, coming together in the interests of the client. There is no place in a coaching relationship for fostering regression within clients, so that they become the 'child' in relation to the coach as 'parent'. Nor is there a place for the coach assuming an expertise in how clients should or should not live their life.

Being trustworthy and trusted is as equally important in a coaching relationship as it is in a therapeutic one. The client has to be able to trust the coach in order to be able to step willingly and openly into the process. This trust is established in the same way as for therapy, by representing yourself honestly and openly, by depth listening and demonstrating that you understand where the clients are in their thinking and feeling. Trust is further reinforced by the confidentiality of the process. Coaching clients, like clients in therapy, need to know the boundary of confidentiality and be assured that this will be respected.

As with therapy, some clients are very rewarding, in that they respond positively to the work. Others, however, can feel more challenging, in that they find it harder to take up the actions needed to bring about change and to let go of old habits. Should a client appear not to be a co-worker in the coaching, you would raise this with them and explore the changes they are looking to make, their level of motivation, and any issues around the coaching process or you as the coach.

The relationship carries similar privileges, as do therapy relationships, in that clients will tell the coach things that they don't share with others. They may, at times, also feel vulnerable and show distress that can feel shaming. As a therapist, you should discuss that in supervision in just the same as you would if it occurred within a therapy relationship.

The orientation of coaching means that the coaching relationship carries differences for the coach and the client. Some of these differences relate to the here and now and future-focus of the work, together with the cognitive-behavioural orientation rather than working with the unconscious processes or deep feeling states. This difference also means that, as the coach, you don't need to open yourself up in the same way to receive this material. When I am in therapy mode, it feels as if I am working from a different part of myself, as if I am opening up my own interior space to give room for the client and the unconscious processes. I don't feel that when I am coaching. I am engaged, engrossed, curious and attuned to the client but I have less sense of being internally available. I am still affected by the client, I still pick up the elements of co-transference and bring them into the work as hunches, but I, too, am more in a cognitive-behavioural place, which differs from my orientation as a therapist.

The different nature of the process, and the reduction in the sense of shame that tends to result from it, mean that it is more likely that coaches and clients can meet comfortably in other settings, including social settings. When a therapist and client meet by accident in other places, both can feel vulnerable and exposed. As a consequence, they often do whatever they can to avoid each other. The nature of secrecy, shame and exposure that can be associated with therapy, and the therapist's orientation concerning their own exposure to the client, can make it more difficult to meet out of context. Often coaches and clients are comfortable meeting each other, and, depending on the relationship, may chat and exchange news with each other. The protection of confidentiality places the coach in the same position as a therapist, that is, it is not for the coach to refer to the coaching relationship or to identify the person as a client to, or in the presence of, others. Issues about meeting are often explored, as they are in therapy, in the first session. This allows clients to tell you how they would like you to respond to them and leaves them in control of the boundaries.

In the coaching relationship, clients are more likely to know about their coach's life and career background than can be the case within a therapeutic relationship. The only rule is that clients aren't paying us for a session to talk about us, they are paying us to work on their agenda as a co-worker on their issues.

I have been coached by people who were, and still are, my friends. I have coached people who have become my friends. A coach and a client might develop an intimate relationship after a coaching process has ended. For example, they might meet up in another setting and realize they had been or had become attracted to each other. There are no rules about that. There is a shared rule with therapy though, that the coach will not pursue their own agenda, or assume power within the relationship nor act in a way that is abusive to the client financially, physically, psychologically or emotionally. If a coach developed sexual or other feelings for a client during a coaching relationship, they should discuss that in supervision in just the same way as they would as a therapist. In the same way too, it would be professionally inappropriate to act on such feelings or bring them into the coaching relationship while that relationship was continuing. As in therapy, it would be wrong for coaches to tell themselves that offering clients an intimate relationship was beneficial to them even if – especially if – having a close relationship may be one of the client's goals. Acting in this way, the coach would be stepping outside the coaching frame, not working in the interests of the client, and would be judged unprofessional. Coaches acting in this way should expect to be reported to their professional body, having broken a core aspect of a code of ethical behaviour.

Developing a coaching package

Coaching can be either a long-term or a time-limited relationship. The most common model is a time-limited one, with an agreed number of sessions over a period of time. Clients use the time to work on particular issues, often related to a transition or key stage in their personal or professional development. A long-term relationship tends to involve telephone coaching and can be used by clients as a means of continuing support and development.

A coaching package details the number and frequency of sessions, over what period of time and at what cost. The client may decide to repeat the package or to extend it by a given number of sessions. A time-limited approach offers some advantages to the coach too, as you can plan ahead and you know when you will be paid.

The nature of the work means that coaching – unlike therapy – doesn't follow a weekly pattern of sessions. Keeping to the same time or same day is unnecessary in coaching. You don't even have to keep to the same venue. You can take breaks when you like and can arrange your coaching client work to fit in with how you want to live your life. You may decide to offer telephone coaching so you don't even have to think about having a consulting room available to work in. In this way coaching can offer some freedom for therapists whose work requires them to keep to a regular and fixed pattern of meetings.

Coaching space needs to provide the same things as therapy space, that is, privacy, quiet, comfortable chairs and accessibility to all wherever possible, including those needing special facilities. If you are telephone coaching, you need a space which is fit for that purpose, so that you can sit comfortably, with a proper headset and won't be interrupted for the duration of the coaching. You will need to ensure too, that there is no intrusive background noise.

The coaching relationship may be brief, perhaps even one session or three sessions over two months. It may last several years and involve telephone coaching, or a mixture of telephone and face-to-face sessions. Clients who have worked with you before might ring up to book one or more sessions to deal with some particular aspect of change they want to work on. Coaching packages therefore vary greatly.

Whatever the arrangement, each session should deliver some shifts in thinking, beliefs and perceptions and lead to changes in behaviour and other actions to take forward the set goals. This can be achieved in ten minutes if the issue is defined. Even in a long-term relationship, each session stands alone and is complete within itself.

Face-to-face coaching sessions can last an hour, two hours or longer. Typically, they are one and a half to two hours in length. This gives enough time to do some work, to move through the coaching process and to arrive at some action. Such sessions are usually scheduled for every four to six weeks. A two-hour session gives clients much to work on. They need enough time between sessions to digest the work and to carry out the actions they have set for themselves.

Although clients can get a lot from one or two coaching sessions, working with a coach for four to six sessions, or more, enables clients to experience coaching in action and to internalize the process sufficiently to coach themselves. Many clients therefore, find a four to six session package over a number of months, perhaps 8–12, to be a useful arrangement.

Coaches need to be prepared to be flexible in adjusting the package of coaching in response to the client's requirements. For example, a client facing a difficult and challenging transition may find it helpful to have shorter and more frequent sessions initially, maybe an hour every fortnight. Alternatively, having the first two sessions closer together, perhaps three weeks apart, could make it easier to invest in the change process. Some coaches also offer a longer first session, perhaps of three hours, to establish an intensive foundation to the work.

Many coaches offer telephone coaching only, or a mixture of face-to-face and telephone coaching. Telephone coaching sessions are usually 30–45 minutes long and tend to be more frequent than face-to-face meetings. For example, the coach might have weekly or fortnightly 30-minute coaching sessions with a client after a longer initial telephone or face-to-face session. By providing telephone coaching, the coach is able to work with people anywhere in the country or world, thus the potential market is not limited by geography. There can also be benefits for clients in that they do not have the added travel time and arrangements that face-to-face meetings might involve.

The number of sessions agreed in a coaching package may be determined by finances as client's funds may be limited. If you are providing coaching to businesses, the number of sessions and the number of clients may be restricted as a means of distributing resources across a larger number of people.

Examples

Margaret works in organizations; she has marketing relationships with the heads of human resources or staff development, and is asked to provide coaching for managers and senior staff. She brings an understanding of the business and managerial world to her work but still works holistically with her clients. She has developed a way of working which involves travelling to her clients. This enables her to have a wider geographical base for her work. She has a coaching caseload of these clients and she also sees clients in her own consulting rooms. She organizes her work so that she sees two or three clients from the same organization or in the same area on the same day and arranges a suitable venue. She prefers to meet her clients outside their office base; that way they can leave some of their work-in-mind behind and aren't disturbed. It gives them more space to work in, a prerequisite of the coaching process. Margaret suggests that sessions are spread out every four to six weeks and negotiates around this with her clients.

Jane took on a coaching client who was based a considerable distance away. They talked about how they might make it work, one option being telephone coaching. The client felt she would prefer to have one-to-one sessions, so they agreed to meet for the first time for a whole day (around five hours), and to review how that was. They agreed to divide the time they had into two sessions, with some space over lunch time for her to make phone calls and relax. When they reviewed it, the client found it a tiring day. Being coached is hard work and it left her with a lot to think about and take forward. However, she liked being well away from her work setting and having enough time to engage with things she often pushed aside. She also found the travelling to and fro gave her space to prepare and to process the coaching. They agreed to two further sessions and then ended the coaching relationship. For Jane it didn't feel ideal, in that it was intensive and was harder to take things step-by-step. However, it enabled the client to do the work she wanted to do to move on. On reflection with her supervisor afterwards, Jane felt that it might have been better to have one face-to-face session, with a series of telephone coaching sessions to continue to move things along. However, she didn't really know whether that would have had a greater impact on the client or not.

Emma lives in England and out of all the options open to her decided to work with a coach she had met on a training programme who was based in America. She really liked the coach and the way she worked and felt that it was a style that would suit her. She calls her coach once a fortnight, at the same time on the same day of the week, and they have a 45-minute telephone coaching session. They've been doing this for over two years. Emma finds this suits her well, it means she gets regular input, she saves things up to talk through with the coach and the coach helps her to keep her focus and motivation. As a result, she has changed her life in all kinds of ways. The coach also now knows a lot about her, they have a close relationship; there is a lot of trust. Ending will be harder for Emma as the relationship has gone on for longer and the coach has become so much part of her life.

Martin only sees clients from his home/work base. They come to see him for a 45-minute introductory session to meet him and find out more about the coaching process. If the client decides to work with Martin, he offers two-hour sessions at spaces that work for the client, usually every four to six weeks for around four sessions. The main part of the session is the first hour to hour and a quarter. He finds that that leaves time to look at actions, reflect on the process and plan the next session. Sometimes they finish in under the two hours; he doesn't drag it out if the main work is done and they are merely filling in time.

Jodie sees her clients fortnightly for an hour and tends to agree a package of six sessions with them, which they can renew if they wish. She finds this gives enough time to work on issues, leaves some space for action to happen, and helps to hold the client in the change process. She usually sees them for a two-hour initial session to include gathering of some information and talking through the coaching process.

John provides career coaching, specifically targeted at working with people going through a career transition. After an introductory meeting, he offers a three-hour career review with up to three follow-up sessions of two hours each, or a combination of face-to-face sessions and telephone coaching. He finds that some clients like the telephone coaching as it gives them a more regular contact with the coach and that helps them to take forward their goals and actions. It also means that he can offer coaching to people in a wide geographical area, as they need only to meet him once and are saved the travelling on subsequent occasions.

Whatever arrangement you, as coach, come to with your clients, you should not allow yourself to become their sole supporter. Remember that clients are resourceful and responsible, they are not wounded and don't need healing. They are after a change process to help them move forward. During the coaching process you will encourage clients to identify what help and support they might need to take a particular action or achieve a goal and who might best be placed to provide that help. This sustains the idea of being helped, enabling the client to recognize that sources of assistance are available and accessible. This ensures that the coach is not the only source of help and support.

Beginnings

As with therapy and counselling, you will get phone calls or emails from potential clients who are hesitant, unsure if you can help them and anxious about reaching out for help and what it might involve. The relationship has started, probably even before this phone call, when the client was researching you and finding out about you. Most coaches offer an initial meeting of 30–45 minutes. This gives both you as the coach, and the client, a chance to get a sense of each other and whether the relationship is likely to work. Many clients will consider two or three potential coaches before making a decision.

The client then will decide whether to go ahead or not and the arrangements will be detailed by a contract. This gives the shape to the coaching relationship and sets out the formal business arrangement. In a similar way to contracts for psychological therapies, the contract covers the model of coaching, the role of the coach, the session length and frequency, confidentiality, fees and payment, cancellations, code of ethics and complaint procedures. It might read something like this.

Model of coaching and confidentiality: Coaching is a fully confidential process through which you can explore your vision for your future, explore the possibilities open to you, decide what goals are the most important to you and the actions you plan to take to achieve them. It will involve you in taking action in-between sessions as part of working towards the goals you have set for yourself. The coaching process provides a neutral and safe space for this work.

The role of the coach: My role as a coach is to work alongside you, supporting and challenging you, so that you can bring about the life goals you want. I will not give advice but will suggest a range of exercises and processes that I hope will enable you to move forward.

Session length and frequency: We will meet for two hours for the first session, then for two hours every four or five weeks (or whatever package you have discussed with the client). We will agree to have four sessions to begin with; we can then take stock, and decide to repeat that pattern if you think that would be beneficial to you.

Payment and cancellations: The fee for this coaching package will be £X, paid for on a monthly basis (further information about the specifics). If you cancel a session less than two weeks in advance, I will need to charge you for that session.

Code of practice and complaint handling: I work to the code of practice laid down by for example, the European Mentoring and Coaching Council (or whichever professional body the coach belongs to) and if you have a complaint please raise it with me in the first instance, and if not resolved, please contact the EMCC/professional body, which can be contacted at the following address...

Margaret tends to contract with an employer to provide coaching to a specified number of senior managers. The package she offers is four two-hour sessions within a six month period. If the client wants to continue, the package is repeated for another six months. She arranges it so that the client pays equal amounts each month for the six months. She finds that helps her own cash flow and also helps clients to manage their budgets.

Martin tends to agree a minimum package of one two-hour session and six one-hour sessions at fortnightly intervals, with payment after each session. If the client wants to continue, Martin sometimes suggests a break of four weeks, then another package of six sessions. Martin also sees clients who want career coaching and he tends to agree a package of three sessions with them. If they want to continue for more, he will discuss with them a suitable schedule.

Emma's coach has an agreement with her for six months of fortnightly telephone coaching sessions of 45-minutes each. At the end of that time the arrangement is reviewed and renewed if required.

Contracting and organizational coaching

Clients often access coaching for themselves or willingly take up an offer of coaching, demonstrating they are active partners in the process. A different dynamic can arise, however, if clients are sent for coaching, or strongly advised to take up the offer of coaching. Both carry a clear message that if the individual doesn't participate in coaching, there will be possible negative consequences for them. This will often place them, and their coach, in a difficult situation. Others who are sent often approach coaching as willing partners and are pleased to have the opportunity. If a client has been sent for coaching, there are heightened issues around confidentiality, the trustworthiness of the coach, and the level of shame experienced by the client. All these need to be explored before entering into a coaching relationship with the individual concerned. As the coach, you need to ensure the boundaries to the work are detailed in the contract you have with the company and the individual.

For example, a manager might be seen to be failing to fulfil the role requirements or have had some development needs identified for which coaching could best provide the means of personal support. This can feel supportive to individuals in that the organization is investing in their development. However, it can also leave individuals feeling angry if they don't agree with the assessment of their performance and if coaching is suggested more as a punishment or last resort rather than a genuine offer of developmental support. Such situations can give rise to complications in the coaching relationship that need careful attention. The strength of the emotions felt by potential clients can be such that the coaching relationship is compromised. For example, clients who are unable to move through their anger or resentment are unable to take responsibility for the situation they are in. This can prevent them from using the coaching process for their own benefit. As a therapist, and a coach, you may be in a good position to enable clients to express these feelings and work through them to enable the coaching to have a chance of success. It is only if, and when, clients realize their job or career is threatened and they want to take action for themselves, that coaching can begin. If they are unwilling partners or unable to move into that place of responsibility, you need to end the coaching relationship.

'What brings you to coaching?' is one of the opening enquiries you would ask potential clients. The answer usually enables you to develop a picture of the process that has resulted in them contemplating a coaching relationship with you. However, sometimes shame prevents clients from saying they were sent, until they feel safer in the coaching relationship. In such situations most clients have decided to take what they can from the process anyway and being sent is not a barrier to the work.

Many clients who enter coaching from an organizational base, sent or not, do so voluntarily as they see coaching as something they can use for themselves. The holistic orientation of coaching allows the focus of the work to be on any aspect of the clients' work, life or work/life balance. It is the clients' agenda. It might be that they use it to work through issues around job change or career transition, which might take them away from their current employer, or they might use the time to talk through home-based issues that they want to change. That is their right as the client. If someone else is paying, they need to know what they are buying and what control or not they have over the coaching outcomes.

There are some specific issues that can arise when taking coaching referrals from organizations, particularly relating to confidentiality and the sharing of information. For example, as the coach you might be working with two different clients, the referring manager who as the sponsor is paying for the coaching from his or her budget and the prospective client. It is important to establish a professional framework for this situation within which you are able to protect the confidential nature of the work.

Endings

As for other time-limited processes, the ending is built into the contract from the start. The most common practice is that the coach sets up the contract for a given number of sessions. That contract might be renewed, but again for a specified period. This means that the coach and the client have the end in mind and the client's goals are set for the process. This helps to bring a focus to the work.

In some circumstances the coaching contract might be open-ended, for example, where the coach and client work together over a number of years, meeting possibly three or four times annually or via a telephone coaching relationship. Managing the ending in a longer-term relationship will be handled in a similar way as for therapy. Both the client and the coach need to recognize the length of the relationship and the issues that ending it will bring.

In coaching relationships where the coach and client haven't agreed a set package of sessions but arrange the sessions one-by-one, the coaching can just end. For example, clients might cancel a session and not rebook, or they might just fail to make the next appointment. They might have moved on, or feel they have got all they want from that particular coach at that particular time. This is a less satisfactory model, as it neither provides an opportunity to reflect on the work together nor allows clients to identify what made most difference to them, and the relationship will end unacknowledged.

Sometimes the coach initiates the ending. For example, if the client appears not to want to engage with the coaching process, the coach might suggest reviewing how it is going and whether it is worth continuing. Or there might be a change in the coach's circumstances, such as a house move. This would be handled in just the same way as for therapy, with as much notice as possible so there is time to accommodate the change into the plan and explore how the client will take the work forward. A coach might also feel compromised by some aspect of the relationship, particularly when coaching in an organizational setting, and decide against working with the client any longer. Again this would need explaining to the client and all opportunities for learning need to be taken.

Each session is complete in itself. Ending a coaching session and a coaching package offer the same opportunities for learning. As the coach you invite clients to reflect on the process:

> What made the most difference to the progress you've been able to make?
> What did you notice about yourself?
> What surprised you the most?
> What are you going to take forward?
> Whose help you might need?
> What will enable you to keep moving in the direction you have set for yourself?

The endings of individual sessions and the whole package are development opportunities for the coach. You will be keen to get feedback from your clients, so that you can continue to develop your practice. A coaching relationship tends to focus on this more than many therapy relationships might. With therapy, the personal development of the therapist tends to be addressed in supervision, or individual reflective practice, rather than in the direct client relationship. Therapists are less likely to ask clients those things that a coach would routinely ask; for example:

> How have we done today?
> How *was* it working with me today/throughout these sessions?
> What did I do or say that was the most useful for you?
> What could I have done or said, that might have been additionally helpful to you?

As a therapist, you may be used to checking out the impact of your interventions on a client, having noticed an unspoken response. You would use this in coaching too, for example, to check out an impression that the client might have agreed to something to please you: 'I have a hunch that when I suggested we used the three chairs exercise you agreed a bit reluctantly. I wondered if I was right about that and if, having done the exercise, you feel your reluctance was well founded?' In this way you are getting feedback for yourself and finding out with clients what had most impact on them.

7 Coaching interventions and techniques

It's not my intention in this chapter to provide you with a coaching tool kit, as there are many other books that do that. Rather, I aim to highlight the language and flavour of the coaching dialogue so that you can assess the similarity and differences in your own practice.

As with therapy, coaching can only be effective through the establishment of a good working alliance, based on trust and rapport and contained in a contractual relationship. Many of the skills needed for coaching are also those needed for psychological therapy. For example, no coaching or therapy can happen without active listening. The type of depth listening that comes from full engagement with, and attunement to, what clients are saying; to their behaviour and feelings as they communicate them. As a therapist, you will be expert at focusing attention on the other, while simultaneously reflecting on process and bringing to mind the next step. Many of those who come into coaching without training in therapy or counselling have to develop this skill. They have to learn how to switch off their own inner conversations and listen for understanding, rather than pondering whether they agree or disagree with what is being said. Learning how to establish rapport, eye contact, mirroring body language and the use of words and images are all part of this active listening and relationship building. When we train managers in the use of coaching skills in their job role, developing the quality of their listening and rapport has a positive influence on other areas of their work as well. They also experience, as do coaching, therapy and counselling clients, how wonderful it is to have someone who truly listens to you.

The ability to establish a working alliance and to listen in depth are the foundation stones for coaching. It is this level of connection that drives the coaching dialogue in just the same way as it does for therapy and counselling.

As the coach, you will be the skilled user of a range of interventions, including exercises and techniques, from which you will select those most likely to be useful to your client. For example, some exercises help explore the *now* of the client's situation while others are useful in imagining a different future or challenging beliefs, perceptions, assumptions and thoughts. The aim is to enable clients to engage their creativity and imagination and, through that, bring about changes in the cognitive processes. Many of these tools will be familiar to you as a therapist; you may already use them in your work.

COACHING INTERVENTIONS AND TECHNIQUES

```
                  Personal orientation
                  Curiosity, intuition
                  Self-management

                        Working
   Selecting and        alliance,         Questioning,
   using                rapport, trust,   challenging and
   exercises and        depth listening   confronting
   techniques           and
                        attentiveness

              Clarifying, reframing, feedback
                    and acknowledging
```

Figure 7.1 Coaching orientation & skills

Figure 7.1 shows the skills and techniques under five main groupings. At the centre are the skills needed for any further intervention and for the working alliance. They are all selected and used within the framework of coaching. In that way, even if you use these processes in your therapy work, you will apply them in a slightly or very different way as a coach. Remember, coaching isn't a different way of doing therapy. It is a different process with a different intention.

Curiosity, intuition and self-management

The curiosity is about the client's thoughts, views of their world, ideas and feelings. It makes us say things like: 'Say more about that' or 'What's most important to you?' with a real interest in the answer. It's not asking question number 15 on the list, nor getting information that we want to use for our own purposes, perhaps to answer a question we have for ourselves. We ask explorative questions because we are curious about the client's thoughts and ideas and want to encourage that same curiosity within the client. This will feel familiar to you as a therapist, as will the use of intuition, that inner sense or thought that emerges as we listen to or engage with the client. Your intuition will often provide an idea that might be useful to the client, either for an exercise or to offer something to the exploration. You might hear yourself saying:

> I have a sense that...
> I wonder if...
> See how this fits for you...

In the coaching frame, these hunches are offered tentatively, thus giving clients a genuine option to pick them up or not. If they appeal, that's great. If they don't, just move on. Clients might come back to them or it might be they were not attuned to their situation in the first place. That's the great thing with your intuition, if it isn't helpful to the client, it can just be dropped. Coaches, like therapists, have to be able to let things go even if they believe they are right.

All the behaviour around self-management associated with therapy relates to coaching as well. You need to manage your own emotional responses, to ensure you are not acting out of your own needs or seeking to implant your own beliefs and thoughts into your clients. As with therapy, you need to make it possible for coaching clients to express whatever they need to say about you or that might have some impact on you. You have to be able to manage your own emotional response or potential identification with clients and keep focused on their process. There may be times when you judge that sharing aspects of your response might be of value to a client or possibly to the quality of the coaching relationship. For example, if a client expressed an opinion or had heard something about you that you didn't identify with, or was incorrect, you might decide to respond in a calm, adult-to-adult way. As a therapist, you are likely to have developed your self-management skills so that you are able to be receptive to what the client needs to communicate, while holding a place of empathy and connection and managing your own internal responses. This will continue to be a vital set of skills within coaching, as our emotional responses will be triggered in just the same way.

Questioning, challenging and confronting

This grouping includes those features that give shape to the coaching process. The first is the use of *powerful questions*. They are powerful because they connect with something in the client and can shift perceptions and beliefs. They can also produce insight or stimulate imagination. You know when you've asked one; it might make the client smile, recognize something, or it might lead to an answer that the client wasn't expecting. Powerful questions do the following:

- Invite imagination.
- Invite the client to do something different.
- Offer an invitation to agency.
- Emphasize YOU KNOW (the client knows the answer).
- Are focused, inviting serious engagement.
- Are short and specific.
- Hold the emotional content, for example fear, while allowing for possibility.
- Enhance the client's self-awareness.

Flat questions are those that give information, produce the same story, replay what is already known, believed or assumed. Closed questions are those that require just a yes or no answer: 'Have you tried ...?' or a justification such as: 'Why did you ...?' where the answer is always: 'Because I this or that, or someone ...' Directive questions include statements that are framed as questions, and carry a judgement or direct the client's thinking or decisions. For example, 'Isn't that unfair on your colleague?' (also a closed question); 'What impact would that have on your partner?' or 'How did that make you feel, frustrated, I imagine?' These aren't powerful; the client knows the answer they are supposed to be giving, so they don't lead to an internalized reframing. A more powerful way of reformulating the *why* question is by using a *what*. For example, 'What was it that led you to take that action or make that decision?' This invites a different exploration, and doesn't involve a justification. Powerful questions are short and succinct, not wrapped up in a lot of words, mustn't be complicated and can be as simple as 'What do you want?' or 'What did you learn?'

Powerful questions are asked from a place of depth listening; if you are not engaged at that level, then the question is unlikely to have an impact. They are the language of coaching, and as a coach, you have to learn it and be fluent. You have to let go of the idea that asking a question is to give you the answer you seek. Powerful questions are intended to provoke a shift of perception, belief or to stimulate insight. In asking questions in this way, with this intention, you as the coach can't predict what the answer will be. Powerful questions are usually unpredictable to clients too; they are unexpected, this adds to their impact. Asking questions in coaching, therefore, must take clients somewhere new, otherwise they waste time and merely recycle old thinking. Powerful questioning is one of the aspects of coaching that can be frustrating to learn but one that can have the most impact. Many coaching books include a range of powerful questions for use in different parts of the process. You will have noticed that most of the examples of cli-dialogue I have given in this book include powerful questions.

As a coach, you will become fluent in the use of powerful questions, and develop an extensive repertoire that you will be able to draw on readily. As a therapist, you may have used some powerful questions in your work, however, they tend not to inform the language of therapy in the same way as they do for coaching. Some therapies use information seeking questions or those that encourage exploration. These can be illuminating for clients as they come to reshape their story or experience. This approach differs from the powerful questioning used in coaching, where your purpose is directed at bringing about a new thought. The proactive function of the coach will often lead you to ask many more powerful questions than you would with your therapy clients. The challenge, often for therapists moving into coaching, is to stop themselves asking the 'why question', or variations of it, or asking questions in the belief that they need more information before they can give a useful intervention. You don't need to have elaborated information before you can help the client shift their thinking and move forward.

Some coaching sessions may just involve powerful questions with no need for other exercises. You will develop your favourites; among mine are:

> What would you rather have?
> If things went the way you wanted, what would be different?
> What would be most helpful to you?
> What will happen if you do nothing?
> What would a good outcome look like?
> On a scale of 0–10 ... how important is this issue/how much energy do you have for it/how committed do you feel about this?
> If your life depended on taking action, what would you do?
> What if it doesn't work out the way you hope?
> What's stopping you?
> What was it that made the most difference last time you found yourself in a similar situation?
> If you knew you couldn't fail (or any other self-limiting belief), what would you do?

Coaching is a proactive process and you will be *interrupting, challenging and confronting* clients should they appear to be talking without focus, if they resist taking responsibility or allow their self-limiting beliefs to dominate their thinking. The client who goes into a storytelling mode, for example, would be interrupted and asked: 'Before we get into the story, I just wondered what it is that you really want to focus on today?' or 'I just want to interrupt to check with you that this is what you want to be focusing on right now.' The free association nature of many therapies means that the particular story being told, and the way it is told, are used as part of the work. Some therapy orientations would not cut across this but work with it as it emerges. Therapists do interrupt, usually to bring clients more fully into relationship with the therapist, with themselves or the therapy work. The nature of the interruption may be different; in coaching, the aim of an interruption is to bring focus to goals and action.

Like coaches, therapists also challenge and confront their clients, to bring behaviour more fully into awareness and to highlight repetitive or destructive patterns. Within coaching, the focus is usually about identifying gaps between saying and doing. For example, if clients talk about how much they would like to do something, or about why they can't do something, as the coach, you might say: 'So what's stopping you grabbing hold of this action right now?' or 'What needs to happen to stop us having this conversation?' The latter was a powerful question asked of me by a friend, also a coach, who had been a valued listener on many occasions. While his listening had felt good, it hadn't provoked any change. He posed this question over breakfast at a mutual friend's house, where we were both staying. It shifted me into action and out of procrastination. At the time, I thought: 'Hey, why aren't you being a good listening shoulder?' but it was the best gift he could have given me.

As a coach, you will be challenging clients in a range of ways. For example, you will be challenging them to take responsibility, to focus and will challenge their self-limiting beliefs too. A coaching client, Deborah, was talking to me in one session about how much she hated a particular aspect of her work; something she had taken on, over which she had control. I realized that allowing her to continue in this vein was just a way of colluding with her view that she 'Had to do it' and had no choice. So I decided to say: 'So, stop doing it.' She looked at me, shocked that I had cut through her story and while she responded with lots of reasons why she couldn't, it identified a choice she could make.

On a different occasion with different clients I have heard myself say:

> Jamie, when are you going to start to take yourself seriously?
> Leah, what has to happen for you to begin to get more of what you want?
> If you are that comfortable with how things are, maybe we should just stop now?
> Is this the story that you are going to tell for the rest of your life?

These were all said in the context of a working alliance, having judged (I hope) that the clients could take the challenge. I felt that what they needed was to cut through old thinking and a stale story so as to enable them to shift their perceptions and habitual thoughts. Challenges can shock clients; for many, no-one will ever have spoken to them like that before. To be useful,

Clarifying, reframing, feedback and acknowledgement

Clarifying

Clarifying and reframing are techniques that will be familiar to you. Clarifying is a way of replaying what clients say back to them or putting together several things clients have said in a way that helps them focus their thoughts and ideas. Sometimes, when clients are thinking new things through, their ideas can appear unconnected and vague. As coaches, we are listening for the connections and can bring some more focus to bear that can be helpful to clients.

In clarifying, it is important that we retain the language and metaphors that clients use, so they recognize their thinking and not our interpretation. Interpretation, or restating in the coach's language, is less helpful as it takes emphasis away from the client. It is only clarification if the client experiences it as such.

For example, Martin is coaching Susan. This is their second session and Susan (a nurse) is talking about what she wants for herself from changes at work:

>SUSAN: Well, it feels difficult. I know I want to stay connected to patient care, I don't want to move into training or management unless I can keep having a lot of contact with patients. I don't really mind, I suppose, what aspect of patient care I am involved in, you know, whether it is chronic or acute care, or elderly or adults. I know that I don't want to move house, I just couldn't go through that again having only moved so recently. I am a cycle ride away from work at the moment and that is just right as I can get home in good time. I really want to be able to use my skills and be part of a good team. I don't mind taking on a training role but I don't want to leave the patients really, as that's what I enjoy most. It's so confusing, it just feels there are so many things that are unknown, I don't know what jobs will be around or which way to go really.
>
>MARTIN: I wonder if it would be helpful if I tried to clarify what I think I am hearing.

[In this way he can also check that he is hearing the right things. Susan nods.]

>MARTIN: I hear you say you want to stay closely connected to patient care,

COACHING INTERVENTIONS AND TECHNIQUES

SUSAN: working with a good team, in a location that you can cycle to, from where you now live, and that you are willing to be flexible about the orientation of the work. Is that right?
Yes, that's it exactly.

In this way Martin has used clarification to bring focus to Susan's goal. He might then continue to work with her on that goal and, together, look at the possibilities open to her.

Reframing

Reframing enables us to examine thoughts or ideas, so as to bring out different meanings or interpretations. It's a way of changing perceptions and it helps by challenging negative interpretations. For example, Peter is coaching Craig who has a self-limiting perception of his boss. Craig believes that his boss is always unreasonable and that is preventing him taking some actions at work:

PETER: What do you value about Bill?
CRAIG: Not much, no, that's probably unfair. He does know his stuff, if you go to him for information or help, he tells you and that's helpful. Somehow that can feel difficult as if I should have known it already, he doesn't give me that impression, that's just me.
PETER: Is there anything else that you value about him?
CRAIG: Well, he works hard I suppose, he pulls his weight in the team and he does try sometimes to be personable, he just doesn't really have the skills for it. I suppose he finds it difficult.

Other reframes could include:

CLIENT: I was in the last two for the post but I didn't get it.
COACH: Well, let's reframe that so we can see what a great job you did to get yourself into the last two. That's fantastic, especially as I remember you said the post generated a lot of applicants.

CLIENT: We were short-listed but it will probably be a waste of time, they'll give the work to someone else.
COACH: Hey! Let's just turn that around so we can celebrate you getting short-listed, they must really think your proposal has something to offer.

CLIENT: I've got no time at all, I can't see how I am going to squeeze in all these things.

COACH: Let's turn that around and look at the time you have got and see how you can use that to its best advantage.

Feedback

Only if they have expressed a desire to hear it, should coaches provide feedback to clients. There are two forms of feedback in coaching, as there are in therapy: appreciative and developmental feedback. Appreciative feedback is that which identifies positive aspects of the client's behaviour, with an encouragement to do more of them. The rationale is that if you identify what you do that works or has a positive impact, then if you do more of it, you may achieve even better outcomes.

Developmental feedback is that which tells you about behaviour that may be stopping you getting the outcomes you seek. All developmental feedback should be about behaviour that clients can change and given in a way that clients can receive it. All feedback needs to be affirmative, that is, contain some positive elements within a developmental framework. Just as for therapy, there is no place for adverse criticism or negative feedback in coaching, for example, 'You are bad at . . .' or 'You always miss the point.' Clients get enough of that in other places. What they should get from you are sensitive reflections, presented in ways that they can accept and with which they are able to do something. It is a way of enabling clients to get a perspective on their behaviour and perhaps gain a different view to add to their own. Feedback should only relate to behaviour or to facts. In giving feedback, we need to own what we say too, thus: 'I noticed . . .' or 'My experience of you is . . .' It should be specific and not generalized, so it needs to relate to a particular situation or interchange.

Sarah had sought coaching as she felt stuck. She had applied for a number of posts, and been short-listed, but hadn't been successful at the interview. The coaching had explored a range of issues about what Sarah wanted for herself over the next few years, about the posts she had applied for and her preparation for the interviews. In that work Sarah identified that she had had some ambivalence about the posts and realized that she had been applying almost out of desperation, and not out of real interest or motivation. In one of the coaching sessions Sarah wanted to explore how she could improve her interviewing technique. Mike, her coach, encouraged her to show him how she sat in the last interview and repeated some of the questions she had been asked in order to observe how she answered them. This gave him some direct information to work with as feedback to her:

MIKE: I wonder if you would like to hear what I noticed when we did that exercise.
SARAH: Yes, anything that will help me.
MIKE: Well, I noticed that your replies sounded well formed and answered the questions. I also noticed that your voice was quiet and I realized that sometimes I had to lean forward to hear you. I also noticed that there was quite a delay between asking the question and your answer. I wondered if maybe this may have had an impact on the panel and whether it led them to wonder about your ability to do the job, or about your confidence.

In doing this, he is providing feedback while adding an opinion that is offered for exploration. He would also add:

MIKE: I wondered if you thought those things might have happened also in the interviews.

By saying this, he was giving her the opportunity to reflect and to judge how similar her answers were:

SARAH: I think it probably was, I know that I can go quiet and take a while to respond to questions. Sometimes, I noticed that the interviews seemed to hurry me up. I think when I am anxious it makes me talk even more quietly and I tend to stumble over words, so I try to talk slowly to prevent that. I know that I know the answer which makes it so frustrating.
MIKE: Would you like to hear what I noticed about how you were sitting?
SARAH: Yes, go on.
MIKE: I noticed that you didn't make eye contact with me as much as you do when we are talking normally together, and that you appeared to slump down a bit in the chair. That's not how I notice you at other times so I wonder if that happens, too, in interviews.

Sarah confirmed that she thought it might. From this point Mike would explore if Sarah would like to use this feedback to work on her interview skills and techniques, and determine what practice might be helpful for her.

At other times a coach might ask: 'I wonder if you would like me to reflect to you what I observe about the situation your are describing?' or 'Would it be helpful for me to share with you what I observe, as you talk about this situation with Mary?' Again clients rarely say it wouldn't be helpful but it is important that feedback isn't given uninvited. It is also important to check by observation and sometimes by asking what impact the feedback is having.

Clients also ask coaches directly for feedback: 'What do you think?'; 'What do you make of it all?'; 'Where do you think I went wrong?' or 'If you were me, what would you do?' Such questions are tempting. However, in answering you would be slipping out of coaching mode and this should be avoided. You need to give yourself enough space between the stimulus (the question) and your response (the answer) to decide whether clients are avoiding taking responsibility for themselves and placing you in a parental role, and what your response should be. For example, the coach might respond:

> COACH: I'm not sure I'm in a good place to give you an opinion on what went wrong, I wonder, though, if it would be useful to explore that a bit together.

Or

> COACH: I am not sure it would be helpful for me to say what I would do and I am wondering whether we could generate some possible actions together?

Sometimes the coach might say:

> COACH: What I notice about the situation you describe is that you seem to end up being placed in a difficult situation by Mary, as if it's hard for you to protect your time boundaries.

Formulating a response question like these is a familiar dilemma for therapists who want to avoid the 'blank screen' of offering no opinions or responses, while at the same time urging clients to work through their own thoughts and solutions. In coaching, the additional intention is to move the client on and to offer the potential for things to be different.

Acknowledgement

Acknowledgement and affirmation are aspects of giving feedback and challenging negative self-talk and the internalized critical parent. As a coach, you will use acknowledgement as an intervention, for example:

> COACH: Mary, I'd really like to acknowledge your courage in stepping into the future in this way.

> COACH: Jane, I'd really like to acknowledge your ability to stand up for yourself.

> COACH: Let's really celebrate the energy you have invested in bringing this about for yourself.

In this way you are naming strengths and positive aspects of the client. You will also champion your clients at times, saying things like: 'Be brave, you can do it' or 'Keep faith, you can make this happen.' Clients need to know that you believe in them and in their capacity. In doing this it is important that you speak from an authentic place; coaching isn't about 'pretending' positiveness, but genuinely believing it.

These types of affirmation are designed to pick up on particular assets clients have, in the perception of the coach, and which (most importantly), are seen to be something that clients are proud of and fit with their values. To do this, you as the coach, need to be fully attuned to clients so that you are picking up the often unspoken or just hinted at messages of self-belief and voicing them back to the client.

Selecting, suggesting and using a range of exercises

Coaching uses a range of exercises and other interventions as part of the process. They are used to support the coaching process and the client's personal development, insight and awareness. The skill of the coach is in selecting those most appropriate for the client and, therefore, most likely to add to the change process. Exercises are offered as suggestions, not as directives, so they are introduced with: 'I wonder if it might be helpful to do an exercise to help bring things into focus/reflect on the learning/expand the area we are looking at ...' You, as the coach, would then tell clients what the exercise involved to give them an opportunity to accept the suggestion or not. Most often clients do accept, as they trust the coach to bring something of value to the process; occasionally they don't. It is important that clients are part of the decision-making and are reminded that they are in control of the process. This is at the core of coaching. The client decides if they want to change an aspect of their life and identifies what would help them do that. The coach doesn't assume that what they think will be helpful, necessarily will be.

For example, the coach might say:

> Jane, as I listen to you, I wonder if it would be useful to use an exercise here. The exercise I am thinking of would involve guided imagery, that is, using your imagination to bring a scene to mind that we would work on together. It may help you develop some different ideas about this situation. Would you like to give it a go and see if it does help?

In this way, as the coach, you are offering something that may help and inviting clients to decide if it would be useful to them at this stage. This maintains an adult:adult relationship.

The exercises and techniques might be paper-based, they might involve guided imagery, movement or offer a way of approaching thinking and reflection. As a coach you'll need to build up your own skills in using a range of different exercises and techniques, drawing on other coaching books and those which apply neuro-linguistic programming (NLP) and similar processes. You will also create your own and adapt exercises that perhaps you already use in your therapy work. There are many links, particularly with gestalt, NLP, and cognitive-behavioural approaches. My aim in this section is to give you a flavour of these rather than give you a tool kit.

Paper-based exercises

Paper-based exercises include both materials sent out in advance of the first session and those used within the sessions. One example would be to draw a picture to represent life as it is, and then life as it would be if the coaching delivered the outcomes sought. Other exercises might help clients identify their values and drivers, those things that are important to them and underpin their life decisions. Other favourites include clients:

- writing what they want to be said at their funeral;
- mapping out their unfulfilled goals;
- reflecting on levels of satisfaction with aspects of their life (home, work, relationships, leisure, money, environment);
- drawing a lifeline showing the ups and downs since adolescence and identifying similarities between the highs and the lows; and
- writing themselves a postcard from the future setting out what they are now doing (at the set time in the future), saying what they love about it and describing how they got here.

Affirmation exercises

You will use affirmation exercises to enable clients to acknowledge and own their strengths and abilities. This enables them to be better protected against their self-limiting beliefs and internal sabotage ('You're stupid, you'll fail ...'). As such, they are reframing exercises too. It will not surprise many psychological therapists how infrequently people are told, and absorb, positive things about themselves and how difficult it is for them to retain positive memories. Affirmations can take a variety of forms:

COACH: Mary, we've been talking a lot about your self-limiting beliefs and about not being good enough, even though you know you are good enough and have achieved much. I wonder whether it might be useful to write out a number of positive statements about yourself on these cards. You would then be able to keep them in your diary and look at them every day. On bad days you may want to look at them several times to remind yourself that you know you are good enough.

Or

COACH: Mary, I wonder if it would be helpful to make a list of all the qualities and positive behaviour you display, so that you can remind yourself of them when you begin to feel negative thoughts emerging.

You may also encourage the client to create an affirmation statement that resonates for them, in that it captures the essence of what they want to be different. Such a statement might be 'I can choose', 'I am allowed to paint' or 'I am resourceful.' Creating such statements may need some work, so that they are short but powerful for the client.

An affirmation exercise is sometimes used to enable clients to embrace and embody a goal. Clients are invited to state the goal as if it had happened: 'I am working in the way I want, within marketing, in a job with people I really like. I am having fun and using all my resources. I have all the resources I need to make this happen.' As the coach, you might encourage clients to say this a number of times, with feeling and conviction, so that it can be absorbed into the way they think about themselves. A particularly powerful affirmation is to get them to state: 'I have all the resources I need to bring about the changes I want.'

When taking a client through an affirmation exercise as a coach, you need to help them get grounded, literally, by having their feet on the floor and feeling the chair, and by doing a short breathing exercise to still themselves and their mind. You would suggest that they say the affirmation a few times every day, perhaps four or five, so that it becomes part of their thinking.

As a therapist, you are likely to have used affirmations but possibly not in such a structured way as you will as a coach. Personal affirmations form part of some therapies, for example, enabling clients to say and feel the impact of: 'I am beautiful ...'; 'I am loveable ...'; 'I am free ...'; whatever they need to feel affirmed. It is the same process but within the coaching frame.

Guided imagery

Coaching uses the power of imagination to help shift beliefs and perceptions. Guided imagery is one of the techniques that you can use. This approach might be used, for example, to create a vision of the future or to work on something from the past. Neuro-linguistic programming brought a wide range of visualization exercises to developmental consultancy and to coaching. Many coaches undertake NLP or other training to develop their skills in using guided imagery techniques effectively in their coaching.

Guided imagery can be used to engage the imagination to do the following:

- create a vision;
- access metaphors or messages not usually available to our consciousness;
- work through a scenario and therefore live it in imagination; and
- heighten self-belief and establish resource memories, thoughts that aid our process of personal change or help create defences, for example, against being destroyed by criticism.

To use this approach, you will need to be a skilled practitioner, adept at working with whichever modality clients prefer for bringing things into their imagination. Modality is a term used in NLP to describe the different ways people do this. There are three modalities: visual, aural and kinaesthetic. People with a visual modality preference bring pictures into their mind; they remember and create new possibilities in this way. They tend to use the language of vision, for example, they might say 'I see what you mean' or 'I have a vision for how I want things.' In working with them, you might ask them to make the picture brighter or bring it towards them. Those with an aural modality, use sounds or words. They say things like 'I hear what you are saying' or 'That rings a bell.' You might ask them how loud the sound is, whether it is stereo or mono, clear or muffled. Those with kinaesthetic sub-modality use feelings or body experiences and might say things like 'I've got a feeling for the place' or 'I need a hand.' You might suggest they explore the shape or sensation of something, how hot or cold it is, what sort of texture it has. Only a proportion of people think visually. Unfortunately, many who do tend to be attracted to guided imagery as a process and mistakenly believe that everyone thinks in pictures. It is frustrating for clients to be asked to create visual images when it is not their preferred modality.

As a coach, therefore, you need to identify which modality your clients prefer. You can do this by asking them and by picking up clues from the language they use. When introducing a guided imagination exercise to a client, you will need to say: 'Bring this into your imagination in whatever way works for you.' In this way you are giving them permission to do it their way.

There are many other exercises that coaching has taken from gestalt therapy and NLP, for example, the two chair exercise. This aims to create an externalized dialogue between two parts of a client or between the client and another person. A variation of this is the three positions exercise where clients talk about a situation, first from their view, then move to a different chair taking the second position of the observer, and finally to a third chair and the position of the other person who was involved. These exercises are useful for helping clients gain a different perspective on a situation; moving to sit in different places acts as a symbolic reinforcement. Where you are using exercises that you may apply within your therapy work, as a coach, you will apply them within a different orientation. This might need some reframing.

Using metaphor

As a therapist you will be familiar with working with metaphor: those that are provided by clients ('I feel as if I am in a prison') or from their dreams, as well as those perhaps provided by you: 'It sounds a bit as if you are stuck in quicksand.' In just the same way, you would use metaphor in coaching as a way of moving clients forward:

> COACH: Is there an image for what you are experiencing?
> CLIENT: It's like a roundabout that is going so fast I am clinging on for dear life.
> COACH: What else is this roundabout like?
> CLIENT: It's colourful but not many people on it.
> COACH: How might you like to change this roundabout?
> CLIENT: I want to slow it down and make it go somewhere.
> COACH: Is there an image that would fit that better?
> CLIENT: Well, I suppose it would be more like a colourful train, with a clear idea of where it is going, with more people in it.

In this way the client and coach have reframed the image and at the same time identified possible steps forward. That is, they could focus on where the train is going, what speed it wants to go at, and who else needs to be on board.

Body work

Coaches can be creative and inventive, drawing on exercises and processes from other sources as well as from the wider coaching field. For example, those coaches who come from a 'body work' orientation, movement or drama, will find new and creative ways to apply those techniques in a coaching frame. Most coaches work with body language as part of reframing and re-energizing clients.

For example, clients might want to work on how they could have more impact in meetings. As part of that you might suggest that they rehearse different body positions to see what emerges. You could invite them to direct you to take up the body position and speaking patterns of someone with low status. Having done that, you could invite them to repeat the process this time demonstrating high status. Most of us know, at some level, what confident and unconfident behaviour looks, feels and sounds like and this process will help clients think about what status signals they give in their body language and speech. Alternatively, you might suggest that clients use their memory to think of a time when they felt confident and self-assured. They would be encouraged to cast that memory in a sharper focus and notice how they were standing, moving, speaking and feeling. You would ask them to describe those things to you in detail. Having brought them back into the room, and out of the memory, you might then ask:

COACH: What did you notice about how you behaved in that situation and memory, and what has been happening in the context you are talking about?
CLIENT: I noticed that I moved and spoke quite differently. I walked tall and had my head up; I was speaking quite a bit, with authority. I seem to find myself sitting rather slumped in meetings at the moment and realize that I don't speak up, that I am a bit afraid. In the memory I had a real sense of people taking notice of me and that made me even more confident.
COACH: How did that feel?
CLIENT: It felt great!
COACH: What resources were you drawing on that enabled you to behave in that way?

In this way, the coach is inviting the client to explore her resourcefulness and how she could apply that in the different situation.

You can use movement to symbolize stepping in and out of a comfort zone and what it feels like, or imagining stepping over a line into the future. You can also use it to free up the thought processes. For example, a colleague and I were working with a group who were training to use coaching techniques. We had engaged actors to take on the role of clients. We used a 'hot seating' process, through which the members of the group took over the coaching process when they had an idea for moving the coaching on a stage. The actor had been briefed to be resistant to coaching interventions so was hard to move on. One trainee coach decided to do something different and suggested to the client that he walk around the room while talking to the coach. Despite himself, in role, the actor was immediately drawn into responding differently. This provided a useful demonstration of how movement can be valuable.

Coaching is a creative process. It offers the opportunity to use a range of different techniques and approaches, and as such, is stimulating practice.

COACHING INTERVENTIONS AND TECHNIQUES 81

When working with clients, if you draw on a range of different types of exercises and processes, it will help prevent you getting into a rut or getting bored by the process. As long as the exercises and processes you use stimulate reflection, creativity and energy in the service of clients' issues, goals, work style and the client isn't shamed, anything is possible.

We can all be repetitive, seeking comfort in familiar processes. This is not in our best interests as coaches, nor in our clients' best interests either. We need to be courageous and innovative, constantly developing our practice and getting feedback on what helps clients most in which types of situation. As coaches, we need to reflect on our practice and be aware if we have reduced the range of techniques and exercises we are using. As therapists and counsellors, this might be a challenge. However, it is necessary to use different techniques with different clients, moving between paper exercises, movement, guided imagery, and other ways of working with thinking processes. Coaching doesn't just rely on dialogue, although it is a talking process, it uses exercises to create the content and focus for the interaction.

Where might you need to enhance your existing skills to work with the full range of coaching skills and techniques? Look at figure 7.2. Rate out of 10, where 10 is: 'I have all the skills I need in this area' and 0 is: 'I am starting from scratch here'. Imagine the 0 is the centre, and 10 at the periphery, draw a line across the segment to indicate your rating:

Figure 7.2 Coaching orientation assessed

THERAPIST INTO COACH

en use the checklist in figure 7.3 to rate your skills as a coach, on a scale from 0–10. See where your strengths and weaknesses are.

Curiosity	
Intuition	
Depth listening ✓	
Self-management	
Rapport building	
Powerful questioning	
Using the client's language	
Challenging	
Reframing	
Clarifying	
Acknowledging	
Giving feedback	
Selecting and using paper-based exercises	
Selecting and using affirmation exercises	
Selecting and using guided imagery	
Using metaphor	
Using body language and movement	

Figure 7.3 Skills checklist

COACHING INTERVENTIONS AND TECHNIQUES 83

Reflective exercise

This is another opportunity to reflect on the similarities and differences between coaching and your therapy orientation.

Table 7.1 Comparison of coaching relationship and coaching package with therapy

Aspect of coaching	*Similar or different?*
The coaching relationship:	
The coaching package: Flexible, face-to-face and/or telephone coaching, frequency and length of sessions	

8 The coaching process

> Action is the antidote to despair.
>
> Joan Baez

So you have taken on a coaching orientation and have a client with whom you have agreed a coaching package. What will you do as the coach in the sessions? Non-content coaching uses a framework for each session and for the totality of the coaching package. This acts as a map for the work. In comparison to some therapies, coaching takes a more structured approach to the work and use of the time in each session. Each session is complete in itself, although of course, themes run through each session. That means that each session follows a similar process that takes the work from the present situation, through goal-setting and ending with action planning. The coaching process has the following phases, as shown in figure 8.1.

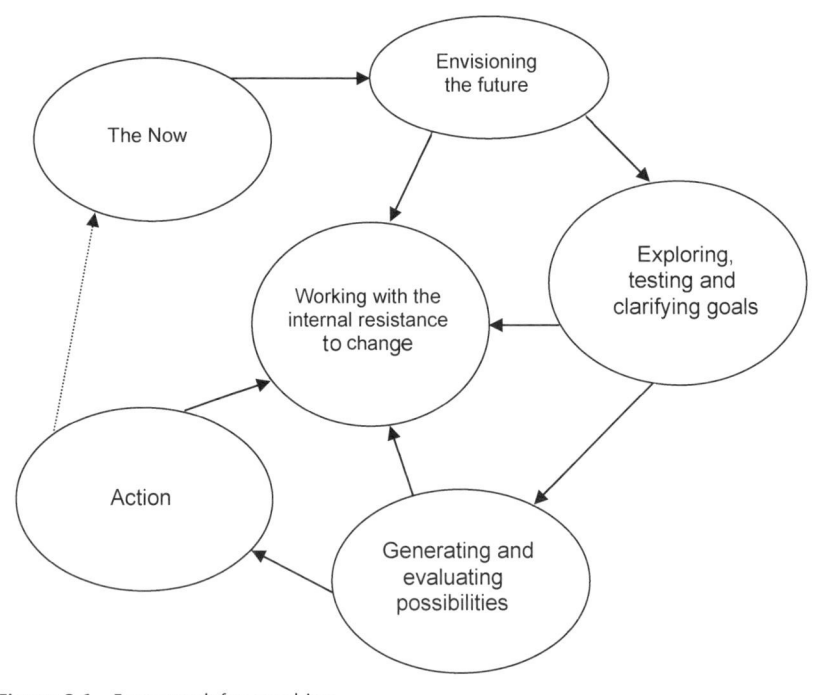

Figure 8.1 Framework for coaching

- *Mapping the now* of the client's present life, what is satisfactory and what isn't. It includes clarifying values and drivers, those things that are important and give meaning.
- *Envisioning the future*: This phase explores, in imagination, what the client's aspirations and hoped fantasies are. It includes working with the answers to the questions: 'What would you rather have?' and 'What do you want to keep?'
- *Exploring, testing and clarifying goals*: The specific aspirations for change that clients wish to set for themselves. This is a detailed part of the process where goals are explored, tested, evaluated and confirmed by the client.
- *Generating and evaluating possibilities*: Ways in which these goals might be achieved, that is, what routes might clients take to get from the now to this desired future?
- *Moving to action*: Determining the actions that the clients are going to take in order to achieve the goal(s) they have set for themselves.

Throughout all these phases, the coaching process also includes working with the internal resistance and capacity to sabotage change. This includes working with the clients' self-limiting beliefs, assumptions, perceptions, particular thoughts that limit what they think it is possible for them to achieve. As the coach, you are drawing on all your skills and the full range of techniques and exercises to enable each client to work through these phases of the coaching process.

This process, from now to action, can operate within a 10- or 15-minute conversation. It is useful for new coaches to practice these short coaching conversations with others, so that they become familiar with the flow of the work. Within a two-hour session the process may be repeated several times as you and the client work on a number of areas they wish to change. The work doesn't always flow sequentially in this way but, as a coach, part of your role is to ensure that all those elements are addressed in an appropriate way within a session and over a coaching relationship. The process is the template for your coaching work.

The coach part of your function is to manage this process while ensuring that the structure does not get in the way of doing the work. For example, new coaches often feel anxious about when to move clients on from one phase of the process to the next and can sometimes move on too soon or in too rigid a manner. Therapists can also find this aspect of coaching a challenge as it puts them in a more proactive role. They can sometimes get stuck in the 'now' phase, being less familiar with moving a client forwards into the future.

Exploring the *now*, the current situation

The first coaching session is often used to map out the totality of the clients' current situation and the areas they want to address throughout the coaching relationship. This work is usually helped by the use of a range of preparatory exercises, sent out to clients in advance, that help them take stock of the current situation. Such exercises might include:

- A lifeline, to map out the highs and lows over their life and any common features between the highs and the lows.
- A life balance wheel that enables a holistic perspective to be brought to the work through the client rating each element in terms of level of satisfaction, for example, health, work, money, relationships, personal growth and physical environment. This additionally allows clients to consider the interrelationships between different elements, for example, health and work, leisure and health or physical environment and well-being.
- Achievements so far and things they would like to achieve in their life.
- Exercises to help clients think about what they want from the coaching and their coach.

You may choose to use these exercises within the session, rather than sending them out in advance. If you do send them out, you need to invite clients to go through their responses with you and to find out what struck them most as they went through the exercises. This mapping process may form a large part of the first session. Your coaching interventions can help clients begin to think differently about their situation and what they might want to be different. Your powerful questions and carefully selected exercises will bring new perspectives to the client.

You would use a values exercise, for example, through exploring a peak experience exercise or questioning. It will enable clients to identify what is important for them to have a sense of fulfilment, so that you can both use these to guide the work. Even in the first session, the process of goals, possibilities and actions will be in your mind, as the coach, as you work with clients towards the actions they are going to take following the session.

All subsequent sessions will start with the present and what clients want to change. You would invite them to explore the aspects of the present so that a range of different perspectives can be generated. For example, if they said they felt stuck, you might ask them to rate how stuck they feel on a scale of 0–10, and then ask them what rating they might want to be able to give in three months time. You might invite them to describe how being stuck is affecting their life. The aim is to clarify with clients what it is that isn't working for them and what they would like instead.

As the coach, you would not explore the history of the situation or the possible underlying motivations. You are not trying to find out *why* this is a problem for them; there is no analytical component to coaching. Your function is to ensure that you have heard what it is the client is experiencing and wants to change. This can be a difficult position for some therapists particularly if you retain a perspective that free association is part of coaching.

Visioning the future

This stage engages clients' imaginations to create a sense of the future life they aspire to. It is a fantasy, but it is not unrealistic or improbable. Through creating a vision or symphony for what they want, clients are already allowing the possibility to formulate it in their minds. One way of doing this is to invite clients to write a postcard to themselves from the future. They can set whatever time frame they want to use; for some this might be two years or more, for others it might be six months. This enables them to set out what they are doing in this future and how they got there.

Exploring, testing and setting goals

Goal clarification and setting is the core aspect of coaching; it is the central vehicle for bringing a future and focused-orientation to the work. Goals are explored, framed up, tested, evaluated and then confirmed by the client. Goal-setting also helps clients to take responsibility for what they want to achieve; reinforcing the principle that they are responsible for their lives and the choices they make.

Goals provide a frame for the coaching work and enable you, as the coach, to ensure that your interventions are in the service of those goals. In this way, goals enable a continual connection to be made between the coaching work and the outcomes clients want. This can be a challenge for some therapists, particularly those who do not work with goals in this detailed way. Some therapies take a proactive approach to specifying goals, for example, cognitive-behaviour, cognitive-analytical and solutions-focused work, and some will explore the client's goals at the beginning of a therapeutic relationship and hold those in mind. However, many therapies tend not to use goals as a core tool in the same way that coaching does. Some therapists may even leave goals indistinct or unfocused with the result that the therapy process can move aimlessly, with the end point blurred and uncertain. Depending on how you use goals in your therapeutic work, goal-setting within coaching may be something that feels uncomfortable and unfamiliar to you. It requires a more planned and focused-orientation to the work; that is, establishing where you want to get to and in what time scale. Some therapists tend to work in a more emergent way, that is with what evolves from the work in relation to the desired direction of travel. For example, some therapies carry the idea that the journey is more important than the destination, which is congruent with the purpose of the therapy and with the preference of the therapist. Coaching works with the destination, bringing it clearly into view and then planning the route. It is a shift in orientation and requires the flexibility of the emergent approach within the framework of future planning. For example, an emergent approach allows for new ideas, perspectives and insights to lead to adjustments to goals and the routes to them. Without the goals, however, the journey might be aimless, with little change being brought about.

The start of a goal-setting discussion may be with clients stating what is wrong with their current context and you asking them: 'What would you rather have?' In this way you are turning negative thoughts to positive solutions-focused ones. The *what's wrong* conversation doesn't change anything; it usually serves to locate blame on others, and by so doing distances the client from them and the problem. It serves to keep clients in a known state, albeit an uncomfortable or unhappy one, where they do not have to take responsibility for changing it. As a coach, you will challenge each client to state their positive 'wants'. There is no point in having a goal that is about 'having less of something' or 'not having or experiencing something' as these just focus on the negative aspect of experience. Coaching is a motivational and empowering process and goals need to be positive statements that help create a sense of a different way of being for each client.

As coaches, we aim to help clients develop transformational goals, that is, goals that carry a 'higher order' of potential and creative options. For example, as a novice coach, you may be thinking about what your goals might be in terms of developing your coaching expertise. It might be that you think your goal is to practice with one person. A more transformational goal could be to find and use as many opportunities as you can to practice your coaching skills and use the coaching techniques. The second goal creates more possibilities and subsumes the first goal. Practising with one person is one of the ways in which the new goal might be met.

The most powerful goals are those that are specific and measurable, that is, they capture a full picture of what is wanted and how clients will know when they have achieved it. Goals are not general statements of intent; they are time bound and carry a high level of motivation and energy for clients. So a goal such as 'I want to be successful' is too general, doesn't connect with behaviour, and has no time scale. Many clients start with these general statements, for example: 'I want to be happy' or 'I want not to have to work so hard' or 'I want to have more self-confidence.'

In working with clients who express such broad statements as these, you would use techniques to encourage them to be more specific, for example, you might ask them:

> What would being successful be like, what would you be doing differently?
> How would you know you were successful, what would be happening around you?

You might decide to use an exercise around imagining themselves in some future situation, as their successful selves: 'Where are you, what are you talking about, who is around you?' In these ways, you are enabling clients to bring a greater degree of clarity to their goal, as we do with a camera lens or radio tuner, turning it to bring focus to the image so that we can see it more clearly with all its detail and colour. You are turning clients towards the future and away from the past and from their inner experience, which is a different process from many therapies.

Bringing a time scale into the goal-setting helps add some sense of urgency to the work and again helps to achieve focus. A client may say: 'I really need to get another job, as this one isn't giving me what I need.' You would work with this to bring clarity to what would be better, what a different job would need to provide to give the client what he/she wanted and needed, what sort of organization it would be (large or small), what his/her working life might be like. Having clarified the goal and filled in more of the picture, you would explore the time frame. David is coaching Ken.

> DAVID (coach): When would you like to be starting this new job?
> KEN: In three months.
> DAVID: Does that feel possible; to do what might be needed to find the new job *and* prepare yourself for it?

This is a feasibility check as there is no point setting an unrealistic time frame.

> KEN: Hm, maybe I am being over-optimistic here, let me think it through a bit more.
> DAVID: What would be a helpful way of doing that?

David and Ken would then explore some of the actions that might be needed and set a time scale that seemed to be achievable, returning to frame up the goal as something like: 'Within 12 months I will have found and started a job which I really want to do, in marketing and within a 50-mile radius of where I live.' This type of goal is arrived at through a lot of coaching work. It also captures Ken's motivation and energy. David checks for that by asking: 'If you could achieve that goal right now, would you take it?' or 'How much energy do you have for doing what is needed to achieve that goal', on a score of 0 (no energy at all) to 10 (so much energy 'I must rush out and start right now?')

If there is hesitation for the first type of question, or the score given to the second type is less than eight, the goal isn't right yet and David would invite Ken to explore what needs adding or changing to the goal.

> DAVID: What is it that isn't quite right yet?

If the goals aren't quite right, then the change processes will not follow. They have to reflect the client's values, those things that are important to him and bring him a sense of fulfilment, and capture high levels of motivational energy. Unless they do, the client will not take the actions needed to bring them about, including taking on and changing those thoughts, beliefs and perceptions that arise to sabotage the process. It is only when the client knows what he wants to bring about, that the negative self-talk emerges which has been holding him back in the past.

Goals need to be positive, SMART statements, that is:

- **S**pecific, not vague.
- **M**easurable (that is the client has clearly identified how they will know when the goal has been achieved, they have a sense of what they will hear, see and feel).
- **A**ttainable (the goals have been tested, are neither unrealistic nor so easy as to require no personal growth or development to achieve).
- **R**esourced (with sufficient levels of skill or capacity to obtain the necessary skills, time, energy, access to help and support), and
- **T**ime bound (a time is set for its achievement).

The coaching process around goal-setting takes clients through these steps so that the goals are clear and carry high levels of motivation and energy. This level of goal-setting is likely to be unfamiliar to many novice coaches and may evoke possible negative experiences within project or business planning. This approach to goal-setting comes from business and it has been demonstrated that the clearer the goal, the much more likely it is that it will be achieved. The more indistinct the goal, the less likely it is to be achieved. Studies within coaching have replicated this experience. If the goals are not really the clients', but those of their parents or others, they will feel like an imposition on clients. That is why it is so important that the goals really reflect what clients want and are the right size to be manageable without being overwhelming.

Goals don't have to be huge, they can be relatively small scale, for example:

- I will set aside a total of half an hour a week to play the piano, starting right now.
- I will rearrange things, within four weeks, so that I work no more than eight hours a day and feel good about it.
- I will do one thing I have never done before, each month, for the next six months.
- I will meet and get to know six new people over the next six months.

Neuro-linguistic programming (NLP) offers a similar but slightly different way of working through outcomes or goals. NLP shares with coaching the belief that to produce the results we want, we need to know what it is we want, and that a good goal or outcome captures our motivation and determination. The framework NLP uses is:

- *Positive*: this comes from the reframing of the negative to the positive: 'What would you rather have?' or 'How could you express that as a positive statement?'
- *Checking*: 'If you could have it, would you take it?' This uses a motivational testing question. Often this results in a 'Yes but ...' or in some hesitation, that provides an opportunity to start reframing.

For example, Martin is working with Jennifer who wants to adjust her work/life balance, as she wants to spend more time with her family and doing things that she wants to do and less time working:

JENNIFER: Yes, I would take shifting my work/life balance as long as I could keep up with the work.
MARTIN: So if you could spend the time you have specified with your family, and on the activities you want to do yourself, and keep up with the work, would you take that?
JENNIFER: Yes I would.

At times, the coach and client may go through this loop a number of times, framing the goal so that it is able to accommodate all the hesitations.

- *Specificity*: The coach helps clients specify who, what, when, how specifically, by taking them through these questions. The coach encourages clients to imagine the situation, perhaps using a guided imagery exercise, and to make the positive statement as specific as they can. The Coach asks: 'When specifically will you spend time with your family?'; 'Which activities, specifically, will you spend time doing for yourself?' or 'When specifically will you do these things?'

- *Evidence*: The coach would suggest that clients imagine they have already achieved this outcome, and invite them to state what they would see, hear and feel. This helps bring a strong image to the desired future state, which is helpful in bringing it about; it also provides a way of knowing when it has been achieved.
- *Own part*: This picks up the possibilities and action parts of the coaching process by inviting clients to look at what they will do to bring it about and to take up the responsibility for effecting the desired change.

Coaching could result in people setting goals and taking actions that are not healthy, ethical nor legal. As a coach, you are in a similar situation as a therapist in this regard. You have a duty of care and a responsibility to uphold the law and need to take up this position of responsibility if a client's wishes are self-destructive, potentially dangerous to others or illegal. This has never happened in my coaching experience. I have challenged clients about the extent to which they appeared to be pushing themselves in a way that was having unhealthy consequences for them, and in relation to possible self-limiting beliefs undermining the goal-setting. For example, a client might have a self-limiting belief about being under educated, and use that to formulate goals around doing a university degree. When pushed for motivation and energy, there wasn't really any but the plan was to use will power, rather than will, to override the low levels of motivational energy to eliminate the self-limiting belief.

Each coaching session starts, after the settling in exchanges, with you asking the client: 'What are your goals for today?' or 'What is it you want to get from our time together?' That leads into a short process on clarifying and testing the goals so that the time is used to take them forward. If you omit this step, the session may have some value and benefit for the client, but it is more likely to meander without really addressing the changes the client wants to make. It can also result in the coach trying too hard to find the motivation, doing too much of the work, while allowing the client not to take responsibility for how the time is used. Novice coaches, including those who are therapists, are often likely to miss out this goal-setting phase, particularly if they are taking up a more passive position in relation to the client or if they are making assumptions about the client's goals. It is less common for therapists to enquire from clients what their goals are for each session; they are more likely, from a free association orientation, to wait for clients to say what they want to talk about rather than what they want to get from the session. In some therapeutic relationships, each session is not necessarily seen as being complete within itself, but part of an ongoing process, building on what has gone before.

Sometimes clients respond to that opening question with: 'I don't know,

I'm not really sure.' As the coach, you must avoid all invitations to direct the discussion. You can do this by asking: 'If you did know what you really wanted today, what might it be?'; 'What would help you most to bring clarity about what you want today?' or you might ask: 'What's around for you as we begin our work today?' The client is resisting directing the work, as the coach your role is not to interpret that resistance, but to bring the client fully into the coaching process. That might lead clients to be able to say more about what is difficult for them. This difficulty may reflect on the coach in some way. For example, your style or approach might be getting in the way of their progress. If this is the case, you need to know what would be better from the client's point of view. As the coach, you want to work with clients in the way that works for them, within the coaching orientation.

As the coach, if you have worked with clients for a number of sessions, you will bear in mind the overarching goals they had set for the work, the actions they took away last time, and the ways they tend to sabotage themselves. You might use this experience to suggest an exercise to explore options or to challenge the resistance and enable them to take on responsibility for their part of the process.

Clients do not arrive at goals superficially. Goals are considered and tested so that they sit with the client's values and sense of well-being. The skill of the coach is to facilitate this process, to work with it for as long as it takes, to refine, test, refine, test again so that the vision can be articulated and felt. Goals are powerful tools so don't ignore them.

Creating and evaluating possibilities

Possibility generation is an important part of developing goals, ways in which the goals might be met and in identifying actions. It therefore comes into all phases of the coaching process. In possibility generation, you work with the client to enable them to generate new possibilities and to break down the power of either/or thinking. Sometimes clients have framed up what they believe is 'the question' they have to answer; for example: 'Shall I focus on developing my dancing or keep on earning money?' By having this question in their mind, they are driven to weigh up one option over the other, as if those were the only two options. As the coach, you might invite them to consider the question 'What other question might you ask yourself?' This can sometimes break the deadlock of the either/or thinking and can give rise to some interesting responses. Most clients have come to coaching because they feel stuck or are not sure how to get more of what they want in life. Their thinking up to now has not produced the needed ideas or possibilities for progress. This is, therefore, an important aspect of the coaching work.

As a therapist you will be familiar with clients finding there are different options open to them, once they have worked through particular feelings or experiences or, when you challenge them. This concept of developing new possibilities is also part of therapy, but in that process it tends to be activated in a less structured way than it is within coaching. Therapy does work with the either/or dilemma that clients can set up in their thinking, and often encourages clients to develop different ways of understanding their situation. In many forms of therapy, other than in more cognitive-orientated therapies, possibilities, like goals, tend to be more emergent. That is, they arise from the work rather than being a specific part of the process. Within coaching, possibility generation is a key part of the process. It is achieved by shifting perceptions and self-beliefs through powerful questions and challenges and through the use of specific exercises.

Ideas-storming

'Ideas-storming' is one of the techniques which may be especially helpful. This is a process that has been used within development consultancy and team development for a long time and has found its way into coaching. It is helpful when the client is finding it hard to come up with ideas or possibilities. It also enables you, as the coach, to add your ideas to the list. Within this technique it is important that all ideas are welcome, especially the wild ones, those that seem so unlikely that they make the client laugh at the thought of them. No processing should go on, until a list has been generated. You need to give time for a second flush of ideas. The first ideas to come out tend to be those that have been thought of before and may or may not have been articulated. The second and third waves of ideas tend to be more creative with new possibilities. As the ideas emerge, they in turn lead to additional associated ideas or slight variations. Introduce the exercises by saying 'I'm wondering if it would be helpful for us to do an ideas-storm here. We'll spend about ten minutes generating as many ideas as we can, it's important we don't "screen" any out before they are said. When we've done that, we'll go through and evaluate each one'.

Jenny is thinking of what she could do to get more artistic expression and stimulation in her life. She has identified that as a goal but is stuck. She is working with her coach, Sue:

SUE: What ideas do you have about how you might achieve this goal?
JENNY (after a short pause): I'm not sure really, I suppose I should set aside some time to paint.

Sue hears the 'I should ...' and wonders if this carries much energy. Rather than test that at this stage she asks: 'I wonder if it might be useful to generate some ideas together of all the ways you might get some more artistic stimulation and expression in your life before you decide what you will do.'

JENNY: Yes, that would be great as I feel really blank.

SUE: Well, let's see how many different ideas we can have together and then we can go back through them to see which ones appeal to you. The important thing is that every idea, no matter how daft or unachievable it may seem on saying it, can be said so we have as rich and long a list as possible.

JENNY: Well, I could go to an art gallery with my sketch book or could go to a life drawing class or could read that book Judy recommended to me.

SUE: You could join a dream group and make a collage of your dreams.

[Sue wants to extend the ideas so seeks to contribute things Jenny may not have thought of.]

JENNY: I could join that group of Ray's that is working with clay or I could go on one of those weekends where you can do all kinds of creative things, so I can get a feel of what I want to do.

Sue is writing down all the ideas. The process continues for around 10-minutes. Sue knows that after the first rush of ideas there will be some silence and it might be tempting to stop at that point but she doesn't as she knows this is a creative pause, the movement from what has already been thought about and what has not been allowed or generated before.

JENNY: You know one thing I've always wanted to do is to do a Foundation Art Course or something like that, it's just never really felt possible. Or maybe I could even do a short art therapy course.

When they have a long enough list, Sue suggests they go through each of them in turn, to see which ones energize Jenny. In saying this she is encouraging Jenny not to close down too soon. In going through the list, Jenny evaluates each possibility.

JENNY: I like that idea but it doesn't really grab me; this one surprised me as I feel quite energized by it; I can't imagine how I would be able to do this one but I'm going to put it on the short list anyway.

This continues until there is a short list of possibilities. Some of these possibilities will have self-limiting beliefs attached to them, for example: 'I could never do this'; 'They'd never accept me'; 'I'm just not good enough really';

'I wouldn't be allowed to' or 'I couldn't afford to'. Possibility generation, like goal-setting, will bring these self-limiting beliefs, and possibly previously disallowed ideas, to the surface. This then allows you to work with clients in challenging ways, shifting these limiting thoughts and in encouraging them to allow other thoughts to have more recognition and value. In this way, coaching works with external, behavioural changes – having more opportunities for artistic expression – and with the internal change in thinking and perceptual habits. Without changing these, there is unlikely to be much external change. This is shared by many approaches to therapy; that is, internal change is needed to produce externalized behavioural change. In coaching and other cognitive approaches, focusing on the behavioural changes through goal-setting and possibility generation forces the emergence of the internal resisters, on which you can then work. Many therapies focus on the internal and perhaps look for signs of change in decisions clients might make in their life. The coaching process takes a different orientation, focusing first on the behavioural changes desired then working with the internal processes needed to bring that about.

This process of ideas-storming and possibilities generation also enables you, as the coach, to contribute your ideas and to add them to the long list. The input from you and the client should be around 15–85 per cent respectively. That is, most of the ideas should be the client's. Your ideas may come from the hunches you have about what may work for the client or serve to bring creativity to the thinking. For example, by offering more unconventional ideas with the aim of shifting the perception of what is possible. I was working with a group of trainee coaches who were considering an issue for one of the participants about how to involve a range of people with particular, and different, interests in a work project. The task was to generate as many ideas as possible for how they might go about this. They slipped into solution finding mode, rather than allowing their imagination to flow. As a consequence the energy level fell. In response, I made two suggestions: 'You could do cartwheels down the road' and 'You could meet in a circus'; both of which were plainly ridiculous. But after the initial shock that I could say something so apparently stupid, the group became more creative about the possibilities and broke free from the stock responses to the problem. Possibilities need to be reality tested, but a process that draws on imagination and the creation of ideas brings something new to the client's thinking. Solutions finding can fall into the trap of seeing that there is a problem to resolve, rather than a different way of behaving that can bring more fulfilment and energy. Coaching tries to avoid this problem-solution formula, even though it is future-focused and, to that extent, solutions-orientated. It avoids this because the formula tends not to be energizing. The client doesn't have a problem to solve, but an inner and outer life to change. It's a different orientation.

Moving to action

The coaching process has moved from now, to what would be better, via possibilities and resistance to goals. It then returns to possibilities and resistance around the ways those goals could be met before moving into the action planning phase. These actions will involve doing things differently, that is, changing behaviour or taking specific actions needed to achieve the goals set. Goals can only be achieved in this way. Actions might include, for example, information gathering or sending, repeating affirmations, connecting with people, accessing other services, skills development and organizing or reorganizing things (papers, clothes, cupboards, activities).

In therapy, clients may state actions they are going to take but usually voluntarily, as it is not part of closing the work within that session. Therapeutic sessions stimulate clients to take action. For example, they may decide to contact a friend, talk about something specific with their partner, visit a grave of a close relative or give themselves a treat. Something has been moved within the session and the action is their response to that change. Even though therapies vary greatly, many therapy sessions are likely to end wherever clients are in their process, not with a particular focus on what they are going to do as a result of the session. In coaching, action planning is part of the session. Clients may well add to and change those actions following the session but they go away with the steps they are going to take before the next session.

In this phase of the coaching process, you would ask the client: 'What actions are you going to take now to move towards this goal?' or 'What's the first step you need to take, however small it might be?' and 'What else?' Coaches often provide clients with an action planning log to complete. An action planning log should include the date of the session, a space for clients to write out their goal and the actions they will take to achieve it.

As the coach, you will also be checking energy and commitment to the actions identified, in the same way as for other decisions. In addition, you might ask: 'How much time are you prepared to put aside to ensure you can take these actions?' and then encourage clients to take a practical look at time scales and how they can build in success for themselves. This might even include suggesting they look at their diary then and there.

Other practical enquiries include: 'How are you going to keep yourself on track?' or 'What will help you most to take these actions?' These are aimed at enabling clients to have the best chance of taking the actions they have set out. Outside the coaching session, life can engulf clients again and spending time on the practicalities can help ground the actions.

Part of action planning is to enquire: 'Whose help might you need?' This could use an ideas-storming exercise so that the client lists as many people as they can think of whose help might be valuable. You might suggest that they build up the list, adding more names as they think of them. They can then go back over each and decide what specific help the person might be able to offer and decide who they will contact as part of their action plan. You will put ideas into the action planning phase, as you do in other possibility discussions. It is the clients' choice, however, whether they want to include your ideas or not.

Holding to account

One of the functions of the coach is to hold the client to account, not to become the critical parent or substitute boss. For example, you might wish to recall from a pervious session and then explore: 'Last time we met you went away with an action plan to do X, and Y, how did you get on?' Depending on the response, you would work with the client to reframe goals in the light of experience, to reframe actions or celebrate achievements and provide personal affirmation. Since coaching is action-orientated, your expectation is that something will have been moved forward from one session to the next.

For example, George is a client in an organization with which Susan, the coach, has a coaching agreement. George wanted the coaching to help him get a better work/life balance and to manage some of his team colleagues better. Susan and George spent the first session exploring his current situation and from that generated some tentative goals. Susan took him through energy and commitment challenges, and he formulated some first step actions that he was committed to taking. When they met a month later George said: 'I haven't had time to move things forward, I have had so much work to do.' He was still, therefore, in the situation which he had said he wanted to move away from. It was true he did work in a highly pressurized setting and the demands on him were considerable. Susan suggested they revisit the goals he had set to check that they were the ones that he really wanted to achieve. If the goals aren't the right ones, the client will find ways of not achieving them. The dialogue went something like:

SUSAN: If your life depended on making these changes, what would you do right now?
GEORGE: I'd stop taking on more work and make myself leave work behind at the end of the day.
SUSAN: What will happen if you do nothing?
GEORGE: Well, I'll get more and more disillusioned; I'd feel my soul was being destroyed; I'd become a robot.
SUSAN: How long can you accept this as the current situation?
GEORGE: Actually, I can't for much longer.

SUSAN: How much longer is that, one month, three months, six months?
GEORGE: I'm not sure, but I think if it's the same in September [seven months away] I will be at the limit of what I can tolerate.

Susan's aim was to see if this helped him access his capacity to take responsibility for himself and to check out the sense of urgency. The dialogue continued:

SUSAN: What would be most useful to focus on for this session?
GEORGE: I think I need to be able to find ways to put myself more central and not to lose myself in all the pressures.

That's what they did for the rest of that session, and the session after, and the session after that. Gradually, they built a different boundary between him and the work demands, working with the self-limiting beliefs, and in so doing, enabled him to explore alternative ways of approaching work/life. In holding to account, the coach is acting as an advocate for the part of the client that wants things to be different, thereby keeping a focus on the future. As the coach you need to present it in this mode, so that clients don't feel blame or shame for not having progressed things but are able to get some learning from it. Even then, the learning might take more time and focus than they had imagined. Clients' struggles need to be acknowledged and a lot of personal affirmation needs to be included in the work, so that they can make things different for themselves. The coach needs to respond sensitively to clients and make judgements on what might be in their best interests at any point (challenge, affirmation, acknowledgement) particularly around moving things forward.

As clients change their behaviour, those around them will respond, sometimes by commenting on the changes in negative tones. This can stimulate anxiety or self-limiting beliefs. One client said to me: 'The trouble is, when I do things differently people say that's not like you.' This troubled her. I suggested to her that maybe she should hear that as positive feedback that she was behaving differently. As that was her goal, it was an indication that she was on track and succeeding. This helped her to shift from feeling bad to feeling good about it, having reframed its meaning for herself.

Holding to account may be an element of some therapies. Where it is, often the goals or actions form part of a treatment programme and have been set by the therapist. The difference in coaching is that the goals and actions are entirely the client's; the coach has no vested interested in them other than working with the client to achieve a more fulfilling life. Therapists may hold clients to account for something they said they would stop doing or do instead. However, that would come out of the work with individual clients;

it is less likely to be a formal part of the process with every client. In coaching, action planning and holding to account are part of the process with every client. You will work in different ways with different clients, judging what might be best for them, but you will always bring a client to action, and follow up those actions at the next session.

Homework

Coaching can involve homework as part of the actions. This would be something the coach suggests the client might find useful to do. It might be to meditate on something, for example: 'What is working?'; 'What makes me happy?'; 'What's fulfilling?'; 'Where do I give my power away?'; 'What am I unwilling to risk?' or 'What is fun?' There are any number of such meditation enquiries, and as the coach you would develop your own bank of questions, selecting from them in response to the client's situation or issues. For example, at the beginning of a coaching relationship you would choose questions that opened up the inner exploration by asking, for example: 'What do I want?'; 'What is choice?' or 'What is it to be present?' You would judge what reflections may help the client to move on. The expectation is that the client will meditate on the question in the space between sessions and you would both work with the responses to that action.

Another form of homework is more of an assignment, for example: 'Count the number of times a day you meet your internal saboteur'; 'Make contact with two people you have been meaning to call'; 'Play the piano for three minutes every day'; 'Use as much paint and paper as you can in the creation of images' or 'Look at some art.' These assignments come out of what has been discussed in the session. They should be achievable by the client and be designed to encourage them to take additional steps towards their goals.

While homework is not common practice in most therapies, it may form part of the process for some. For example, in couples work, homework is given for the clients to work on together between sessions. Where this is not something you are used to doing, it might require you to practice more so that you get some feedback and can feel comfortable with this part of the coaching process.

Some coaches also suggest that clients keep a reflective log, writing for 15 minutes or so a day about what is in their mind and what they are noticing as they take their goals forward. Many clients find it helpful to have half an hour reflective period shortly after the coaching session to write up what they learnt, what they noticed, thoughts and feelings and the actions they are going to take. These activities help to keep clients on track and reinforce the need for continual personal work to bring about change.

Challenging resistance

A key part of the coaching process, in each phase, is that of working with the internal resistors to change. These arise as a result of the close focus on goals, possibilities and actions. The internal beliefs that have caused the client to end up in an unsatisfactory life position, surface and, unless challenged, will sabotage change. Achieving the internal change needed to support external behavioural change is a core aspect of coaching. Whenever you are working with personal change, you will meet the internal resistance to that change, something you will be familiar with as a therapist. In coaching, this work is called working with self-limiting beliefs and the internal saboteur. The thinking processes are seen as self-limiting to the extent that they prevent clients from accessing their full resources and potential. As a therapist you will have a view on how these have been created and maintained. You may call them the parental injunctions or the negative super-ego or script, and are likely to work with these factors already as an important part of the therapy process. In coaching, you will not be interested in diagnosing or interpreting how they have come into being. Your role is to focus clients on challenging and changing them, where they want to make changes. Most clients do, but it is their choice. As with therapy, coaching clients hold onto these beliefs and it can take repeated work to reduce the power that the thoughts and associated feelings have over a client's life. These thoughts, beliefs, assumptions and perceptions, have been built up over the client's life and, as within therapy, they are remarkably resistant to challenge. They are justifications for keeping things just as they are, to keep the levels of dissatisfaction the same and to avoid disobeying the negative inner voice.

The expression of these self-limiting beliefs will be heard as statements, for example:

> I couldn't possibly do...
> I can't do that because...
> I couldn't afford to do that...
> I'd feel stupid doing that...
> X would never let me...
> You don't understand, I have to do what I am doing now...
> I'm terrible at...

The internal saboteur speaks to clients with their own voice. For example:

> You're stupid.
> You'll never get this right.
> You will fail whatever you do.

You're too fat to be successful.
You don't deserve to be happy.
You bring misery to everyone.
No one can love you.
You're nobody, no one is interested in you.

The self-limiting beliefs and this internal saboteur will be familiar to all therapists, you will have heard them spoken many times in your consulting room. The internal saboteur, particularly, usually carries a huge amount of pain for the client and can be shaming to speak of. Clients talk of it as an internal force that makes them do things or tells them they are useless, stupid, a waste of time. The voice is always negative and attacking. It is often experienced as something that is 'non-me' and has 'power over me'. Some writers on coaching, for example, Richard Carson in his book, *Taming Your Gremlin* (1987), refer to this as the Gremlin. Many coaches now use this term with the client, and enable them to enter into dialogue with this being, to give it an image, isolate it and take back some control over its impact. This is not very different from how some therapists might work with negative self-talk; enabling clients to experience a dialogue with the internalized voice, to distance themselves and prevent themselves being overwhelmed by it.

We all have our own versions of both the self-limiting beliefs and the internal saboteur. As a coach, you need to know what yours are. You may already be aware of them and it is likely they will surface as you make goals to change aspects of your life, perhaps to include a shift to coaching.

As a coach, you need to develop an acute hearing for self-limiting beliefs and for the voice of the internal saboteur. Challenging and changing them or reducing their impact, makes the difference between the client changing or not.

Self-limiting beliefs

On hearing what sound like self-limiting beliefs, you will need to check with clients and ask if they still want to carry that belief about themselves. If they say 'Yes', you might ask: 'What is it about the belief that is valuable to you? In what way does it help you?' That might lead to reframing it as a more positive statement that allows for more possibilities to flow. If they say 'No', you have a range of options to draw on. You could challenge them, for example, by asking: 'What's the worst thing that could happen?' or ask them to restate an 'I can't' statement with an 'I won't', and work from that point. Alternatively, you could challenge the generalization that is usually part of the belief. For example, to a client who said: 'I am hopeless at selling', you could ask: 'Have you ever been effective in selling something, however small or in whatever way?' If the client can recall a time, you would ask for a description of that time and where the resourcefulness had come from. This takes the client into contact with that resourcefulness, and from there, you can ask how that resourcefulness can be transferred to the new situation.

Another way is to suggest that the client states the opposite of the self-limiting belief. This can be useful although it is important not to work on an unobtainable opposite and word it in a way that is acceptable to the client. Sue is coaching Kate in this following example. Kate has said she is bad at making presentations, that people look bored.

> SUE (having checked the client wants to work on this belief and is willing to do this exercise):   So, supposing you state the opposite of that self-limiting belief?
> KATE: Well, I suppose that would be: 'When I make presentations I am interesting and engaging.'
> SUE: Can you say that again, with feeling?

Sue will encourage Kate to say it several times, and to reframe it if it isn't quite right, so that it carries meaning for the client:

> SUE: If you could believe that your presentations were interesting and engaging, how would that feel?

In asking the feeling question, Sue wants to check what feeling is associated with the new thought. If it is a negative feeling, she would do more work on the statement and keep checking the feelings associated with the new thought:

> KATE: Scary, but good, too.
> SUE: If you were able to act as if this belief was true, and were able not to feel too scared, what would you be doing differently?

Sue would encourage Kate to be specific about those things, including what she would be doing, saying and feeling. She would then bring the possibility into Kate's imagination so that she was able to have a sense of what it might be like to work with a different belief. In this way, she has worked with Kate's imagination to create a new possibility.

A coach could also use a guided imagery exercise to bring a possible scenario to mind, to work it through and have an experience, albeit an imagined one, of living with a different belief. Jake is working with a client, Martha, who has a goal to set herself up as an independent consultant working in information technology. She has a goal to establish herself in the organizational market. She hasn't worked for herself before and has some feelings about that. In working through her goals, she raised the following self-limiting belief:

MARTHA: I don't think I would ever be able to sell myself to an organization.
JAKE: Would you like to do some work on that using your imagination?
MARTHA: Yes.
JAKE: OK, Martha, if it helps you, close your eyes and just play the scenes through in your imagination in any way that works for you. At any time you can call a halt. Is that clear?

He gets Martha's agreement. He has worked with Martha for a while and knows that she uses a visual modality for her imagination.

JAKE: Can you imagine yourself getting ready to go to a particular organization to meet the director of information or the person who you need to sell to?
MARTHA: Yes, I'm putting on a smart suit and have a decent briefcase.
JAKE: What are you feeling?
MARTHA: I'm feeling a bit nervous but the suit is making me feel more the part.
JAKE: OK, so can you imagine yourself arriving at reception?
MARTHA: No, I feel stuck in my car.
JAKE: OK, stay in the car for now. Just sit there until you feel ready to open the door and step out. [Jake realized he had been taking the exercise too fast and slowed it down. Pause.]
MARTHA: I'm taking a deep breath and opening the door. I'm out of the car and locking the door.
JAKE: Good, how's it feeling?
MARTHA: Actually, it's OK.
JAKE: Are you ready to walk over to the door of the building?
MARTHA: Yes, I'm going there now. I'm through the door and can see the reception ahead of me.
JAKE: Take your time, when you're ready go over to reception...

Jake takes Martha through imagining going up to reception, introducing herself and finding her way to the office of the person she needs to see. During that process she realizes she doesn't have any business cards, so Jake takes her, in her imagination, back a few steps so she can replay the scene with her business cards.

JAKE: So when you are ready, open your eyes and fix your gaze on that picture on the opposite wall. Really feel yourself back in this

	room with me. Feel your feet on the floor and the solid ground beneath them. [It is important with visual imagery, to bring the person back to a grounded position].
Jake:	So what did you get out of that exercise?
Martha:	Well, it was good to imagine myself doing it as it feels a lot easier, although still a bit scary.
Jake:	What else? [prompting her to talk about her experience].
Martha:	Well, I realized I would have to put some energy into setting it up, phoning, explaining what I had to offer and asking if I could call in to meet her. Then realized I would need business cards and some leaflet or something. I realized that I would have to have something clear to present to her. How likely is it that someone heading up IT would agree to meet me, do you think?
Jake:	Well, what does your experience tell you? [avoiding the invitation to be placed in the expert position].
Martha:	I guess, it will depend, some might and some might not, I suppose.
Jake:	What else do you think might make a difference?
Martha:	I suppose if I said I'd only take up no more that half an hour of their time, and ensured I would, that might help? Also if I could use someone's name that meant something to them.

They continue working in this way. Then, at the end of the session:

Jake:	How is this feeling now? What do you feel about offering your expertise to organizations?
Martha:	It feels possible. I'm not going to rush it though; that's what I've realized. I would rather plan it over a longer time and enable myself to keep confident than rush ahead. It's going to be a big shift for me. I'm going to talk to some other people who've made this shift and find out what worked for them.

This exercise challenged Martha's initial self-limiting belief and offered a sense of what it might be like to overcome it. She remained cautious but had a better sense of what she would need to do to market herself to organizations. She worked with Jake in future sessions to determine whether this goal was the one she wanted and whether it fitted with her values. The issue then became how to get what she wanted, for example, what her selling strategy and marketing plan might be. Having challenged her self-limiting belief, it became possible to explore other options.

Some self-beliefs may reflect self-knowledge. For example, someone might say: 'I'm not good at detail', which might be true. However, to say: 'I'm no good at detail and therefore I would never succeed in business', is self-limiting as it negates the possibility of setting up a business. If the client has a goal to set up a specific business, and there are problems with handling detail, the question becomes how to overcome that. One option is to improve the capacity for detail. However, there are others, for example, to involve people who are naturally good at detail. Beliefs become self-limiting when they are used to justify why a client can't do something or shouldn't even contemplate something. They limit the development of learning and experience.

You will also hear clients express beliefs about others that are self-limiting to the client and to the quality of the relationship they might have with that other person. For example, the client might say, 'She wouldn't ...'; 'He isn't able to ...' or 'She's not capable of ...'. Working with these self-limiting beliefs is part of being able to imagine, and bring about, a different way of being together. This also helps clients change how they have set up this system of relating, if that is what will enable them to achieve their goals.

As a coach, you will employ a range of techniques for working with clients in these ways. Each session is likely to throw up a new or known self-limiting belief. You will work with them over and over, until the power of these beliefs are reduced and alternative self-talk is in place.

Challenging the grip of the internal saboteur

As with some therapies, coaching works with the internal saboteur by using techniques that help clients to protect themselves from internal attack. A coaching approach might include calling this self-talk the internal saboteur or critic, so that clients can recognize it for what it is, and that it isn't the truth. This capacity to identify, and name it, begins the process, as in therapy, of putting space between the stimulus (the negative self-attack) and the response (often feelings of despair and failure). This helps clients put a boundary around this entity and it can become something they can then engage with, as if it were a separate being. This enables clients to have different choices in terms of the response they make to the saboteur. One coaching technique is to invite clients to create an image for this being that does the attacking, to identify what colour it is and even to give it a name. In this example, Martin is coaching Jane.

> MARTIN: I wonder what image you would like to give this voice that tells you such negative things?
> JANE: It's a Gollum-like creature, but dark green.
> MARTIN: Does it have a name?
> JANE: Yes, it's called Slimy.

Martin then has some choices, he could talk Jane into an imagination exercise in which she creates the image and then reduces the size of it until it is tiny and becomes a speck of dust, and encourage her to repeat that several times. Or he could invite her to enter into a dialogue with this object, perhaps using two chairs. In this way he will help her rehearse what she might say to Slimy next time it speaks to her. He might encourage her to practice that several times. He might also take her through an affirmation exercise that builds on that, for example, 'I am successful, I am resourceful, I am a good person' and encourage her to repeat that several times every day.

Working with the internal saboteur in these ways often evokes in clients some memories that appear to be connected to the negative talk. These could be school memories or parental voices. It might be the first time they have made a connection between the two. As with therapy, this can come as both a shock and a relief, and can bring some deep emotion to the surface. As a therapist, this will be familiar territory to you. As a coach, you will need to stay in coaching mode and not be tempted to return to a therapeutic relationship.

Again, as with therapy, combating this internal saboteur in coaching is not a quick and easy task as it springs from a deep internalization of experience. The coaching approach is not to 'coach the gremlin'; that is, not to engage with what 'it' says and challenge the reality of it, but to enable the client to put in place some strategies that will lead to it being disempowered.

Structuring sessions

Managing the coaching process requires you to bring together all aspects of the coaching orientation, framework, relationship and contract together with the application of skills and interventions to support that process. The coach is the person who holds that together within the session and throughout the coaching relationship with the client. That is the expertise that you bring to the coaching relationship. Just as with a therapeutic relationship, you are responsible for managing the process as well as yourself.

Coaching differs from some therapies in that the coach is also holding in mind the process of moving from the now, through goals, to actions. The aim for all coaching sessions is to bring clients to the point of determining the actions they will take to progress their goals. Sessions normally follow a similar pattern: beginning, core and closing:

Beginning:

- Greetings and settling in; re-establishing contact.
- Reflecting on learning and discovery from homework or actions.
- Bringing focus to the goals for the session; being clear with clients what they want from the session.

Core of the session:

- Describing the present and identifying what the client would rather have in the future.
- Exploring, testing and setting goals or outcomes.
- Exploring and testing possible actions.

In the process, you will be identifying and working with:

- Those things that are of value to the client, what they need for a sense of fulfilment.
- The client's internal resistance and saboteur.

Closing:

- Action planning.
- Homework.
- Reflection and feedback to the coach.
- Ending.

This can be achieved in whatever time the session offers. In some sessions, you might go through the core elements of a number of different goals. The amount of time spent on each element will vary. All sessions need to come to an action planning focus towards the end of the time available, even if there is more work to do on goals, possibilities or resistance. Clients could add doing work on those to their action plan.

The structure of sessions, therefore, reflects the coaching process, with the addition of managing the beginnings and endings. The beginning of a coaching session may differ from therapy in that you will invite clients to focus on what they want to get from the session, and not leave them telling a story for too long before you interrupt. You might also interrupt a story to find out how they got on with their actions and the homework. In this way, you will be stepping in, perhaps earlier than you might in a therapeutic process, and with a particular aim of generating the material for the session. You will want to get to this early enough in the session, to give you and the client time to do some proper work on those desired outcomes.

In the same way as for a therapeutic relationship, the first coaching session is concerned with setting up the contract and way of working. For example, you would include a discussion and confirmation of the contractual and confidentiality framework, would explore any boundary issues, introduce more about yourself, find out about what matters to the clients, and what has brought them to this point. The final session would also reflect on the whole process and what had been valuable and had been learned. It would also acknowledge the ending of the relationship.

Within each phase of the session you will select and use interventions, techniques and exercises that you judge will be of most value to the client.

Table 8.1 Techniques used in different stages of the session

Stage of session	Possible technique or exercise
Beginning	
• Greetings and settling in; re-establishing contact	Rapport, establishing the relationship
	Depth listening, curiosity, intuition
• Reflect on learning and discovery from homework or actions	Self-management
	Powerful questioning; challenging, confronting, interrupting
• Bring focus to the goals for the day; be clear with clients what it is they want from the session	Action learning
	Holding to account
Core of the session	
• Describe the present and identify what the client would rather have in the future	Depth listening, curiosity, intuition
	Self-management
	Powerful questioning, challenging confronting
• Explore, test and set goals or outcomes	Reframing, clarifying
• Explore and test possible actions	Listening for self-limiting beliefs and the internal saboteur
	Ideas-storming
	Goal-setting
	Commitment and energy testing
	Values exercises
	Affirmation
	Feedback
	Guided imagination
	Use of paper exercises
	Metaphor
Closing	
• Action planning	Depth listening, curiosity, intuition
• Homework	Self-management
• Reflection	Powerful questioning, challenging, clarifying
• Ending	Action planning
	Commitment and energy testing
	Selecting homework
	Action learning
	Inviting and accepting feedback
	Closure and breaking rapport
	Ending

Table 8.1 shows the different interventions and techniques you might use at different phases of the session.

As coaches use different lengths of session time, it is difficult to be precise about how long each part should take. For a one and a half-hour session, the timings might go something like:

> Beginning: 10–15 minutes
> Core of the session: one-hour
> Action planning, reflection, homework, ending: 15–20 minutes.

It is up to the coach's judgement to manage the time, to get to some actions, while also honouring and respecting what clients want to work on and ways they might find it helpful to do that. Clearly, it would not be appropriate to move clients on too early and equally it would not be helpful to fall into a storytelling mode or getting stuck in processing unless it directly relates to moving the work forward. Judgement comes with practice, feedback and reflection. If you were working with a client for a shorter length of time, you would only be able to work with one or two particular things the client wanted to change. In a longer session, you would be able to address perhaps three or four small goals or one large one and a couple of smaller ones.

9 Barriers, problems and challenges

In common with other developmental processes, coaching is not always straightforward; problems and challenges may arise for coaches. However, they are likely to be experienced more frequently by novice coaches and those who are not properly attending to their practice and professional development. Some of these problems can also arise in therapy relationships and will already be familiar to you. Others are more associated with coaching. There are also traps or challenges that, while shared with some novice coaches, can result from therapists' inability to shift fully from therapy to coaching practice.

Problems and traps for all novice coaches

Working too hard

Coaches can sometimes find themselves working too hard in the sessions. For example, by doing more of the talking and encouraging in an attempt to pull clients more into the process. When this happens, the client's energies tend to be flat, while the coach's energy is towards the hyperactive end of possibilities. This can occur if clients have lapsed into passivity and don't take up their responsibilities as a participant. It can also happen if something has made you, the coach, anxious about what you are doing, or how you are doing it. Working too hard is more likely to happen if you haven't ensured that clients have sufficiently clarified their goals for a session or for their life changes. If ever you become aware of doing most of the work, it indicates that you have moved into parent mode. Therefore, you will need to review your position, re-establish your client focus, invite some reflection on the coaching experience and restart the process from there.

Missing the client

By this I mean the coach's questions or clarifications appear not to connect with the client. This will happen occasionally with some clients and will be familiar to most therapists. The response is the same within coaching as it is within therapy; you need to let it go and re-engage with the client. If it is happening more frequently, it could be that you are listening at a superficial level. That is, you appear to be listening but you are also conducting an internal dialogue, for example, about what the client is saying, or what you might do next. This can happen with novice coaches as they try to hold the framework, process, techniques and exercises in mind. If this happens, you need to deepen the quality of your listening so you are more fully engaged with your client. It could also be that you have been offering interpretations or re-clarifications using your language and not that of the client. The solution is the same, deepen your listening and that will connect you with the language and imagery used by the client. If you became aware you had been doing this, then just acknowledge it, as you might in a therapeutic relationship, and move on.

It could be that clients haven't sufficiently described the issue or what they want. If that is the case, questioning can help. For example, by asking: 'Tell me more'; 'What do you make of it?'; 'How does it look to you?'; 'What do you mean?' or 'What other aspects can you think of?' In this way, you are getting more information to connect with your client. You will know from your therapy work that some clients are fluent in talking about their life, while others find it harder, being more cautious about what they disclose. The techniques you have from your therapy work, for responding to these differences in levels of extroversion and disclosure, are directly transferable to the coaching setting.

Confusing wishes with goals

Clients need to be able to create wishes. However, wishes aren't goals: goals are things we are committed to bringing about for ourselves. They need working on, testing, evaluating and enacting. Though goals may well be developed from wishes, it's important that coach and client confine themselves to working with the goals. Coaching tends to get confused if goals aren't clear or sufficiently grounded. So if someone says: 'I want to grow cabbages'; it needs to be seen as a wish or possibly a metaphor rather than a goal. You need to be careful not to respond to the wish as if it were a goal, but to examine its meaning and what it might say about the client's goal. For example, growing cabbages may represent a wish for a slower life with a different connection with nature or the earth, or, quite simply an aspiration to grow special varieties of cabbages or plants.

Telling

I have been at pains throughout this book to emphasize the non-directive nature of coaching. However, there may be times when it is appropriate for you to adjust your approach, particularly if clients are thinking in ways that might be harmful to them.

As a therapist you will probably be familiar with this shift from a non-directive to a directive stance when protecting the client seems to be necessary. Many coaches have to learn to be non-directive before they can take up telling a client to stop doing something at an appropriate point. For example, if a client is locked into the internal sabotage and a negative spiral of thoughts: 'I'll never be any good, I can't get this right, I am not achieving anything ...', you may need to step in and say: 'Stop this. This is destructive. This is not in your best interests.' Or if a client is clearly struggling with work and not feeling well, you might say: 'This can't continue, this is damaging to you. You must take a break.' A client may also tell you about a serious health problem that's not receiving proper attention and the coach might say: 'This is important, you need to attend to it.' When said, it can sound intrusive, as the level of direction in the statement is strong and different from most coaching interventions. It needs to be used rarely and with caution and only when you are convinced it is in the client's best interests. This will be familiar to therapists and you will already be practised in it, so it is less likely to be a problem for you than for other novice coaches.

Forgetting that coaching is non-directive (other than when telling is important)

This can happen if you think, usually misguidedly, that you have some knowledge or experience that is relevant to the client. This may lead you, invited or uninvited, to tell the client about it, thus using up the client's valuable time. Alternatively, you might fall into asking questions for information, rather than those that move the client on. Sometimes you might assume a problem-solving mode and push for a solution even though all the signs from the client are that this isn't helping. All these interventions tend to stop clients talking, as they transfer the focus for the work from client to coach. It can appear that clients are there for the benefit of coaches and not the other way round. If you catch yourself doing this, just stop and re-engage with the client. You may choose to raise it with the client, for example, by saying: 'I realize I have been asking you a lot of questions, where would you most like to bring the focus now?' In that way you are returning control to the client.

Coach fatigue or boredom

These present similar barriers to coaching as they do to therapy. Coaching can be tiring and the coach's life may be demanding. However, just as in providing therapy, you need to be able to manage your energy and be sure you balance your life, and re-energize yourself through exercise, leisure and relationships. If you feel bored, that might indicate something about the process. Perhaps your client is bored too, or is presenting him/herself in a flat, uninteresting way. It might be that you have become mechanistic in your practice and need to remind yourself of, or refresh your use of, different tools and techniques. If clients are boring, it might be as a result of how you are working with them. Alternatively, it might be how clients communicate and they may be open to feedback about it, especially if one of their goals is to increase their network of friends or colleagues. As the coach, you need to reflect on the possible causes of the boredom and fatigue, take action on those that you need to, and in the session re-engage with the client. For example, you might interrupt a client who is talking in a flat and boring way by summarizing what you think they are saying. The client can correct you if you get it wrong. Alternatively, you might pose a question such as 'What's the real issue here?' or 'What's the issue for you?' This latter question is helpful if the client is talking about someone else in the story.

Environmental interruptions

Interruptions to a coaching session are as disruptive as they would be to a therapy session. Your responsibility as a coach is just the same as a therapist. You need to ensure that the venue is private and suitable, that is, with comfortable seating and warmth. If you are coaching in an organization it is always better to see clients in a neutral room away from their workplace, so they are not interrupted and can have some space after a session before returning to work. Other useful tips include:

- Don't arrange coaching in a hotel foyer, even if it looks like you could be private in the corner.
- Don't arrange a room with glass doors or windows onto a car park unless you can curtain them off and still have enough light (people are very curious when they pass by).
- Do carry out telephone coaching in an appropriate venue, with a headset, and not just where you happen to be on your mobile phone.

Not being honest

Sometimes client's issues will touch some of your own. For example, you might also be struggling with a work/life imbalance or have an experience which is similar to the client's. Clients might also tell you something that disturbs you by challenging some of your values. In these situations, as within therapy, you need to be able to be honest with yourself about the impact the client's issues are having on you so you do not act on them out of a lack of awareness. By giving yourself the space to reflect, you can decide which options you have open to you. One option might be to be honest with the client. You might say: 'What you are saying is having quite a resonance with me. I've experienced a similar situation and may need to check with you as we work on this that I am not letting my issues influence your thinking. Do tell me if you have a sense that that might be happening.'

Staying with the facts and ignoring feelings

This is unlikely to be a trap for a therapist. The trap for you might be more that you focus only on feelings. However, as coaching uses thoughts to bring about change, it is possible for feelings to be left out. This is not the aim of coaching. As a coach, you would be checking with clients what they are feeling as part of the work and the exercises. You will want to find out if goals or reframed self-beliefs are connecting with positive feelings. For example, you want to know what feelings are provoked when clients talk about their thoughts and their situation.

Common challenges and traps for therapists moving into coaching

In addition to the above problems that can occur for any coach, there are some particular traps that therapists can fall into, depending on their practice orientation.

Being too inactive

When we train psychological therapists in coaching techniques, we notice that they often appear passive and slow to challenge or intervene, in comparison with those from different backgrounds. We notice that therapists tend to stay in listening mode for longer and appear to be less proactive. It is possible that your activity is internal and that you are waiting for a suitable time to make an intervention. Our sense is that therapists are more familiar with giving clients a lot of time to tell a story, to meander to a point. This is congruent with a free association approach to the work, within which the therapist is looking for themes and patterns to emerge.

As a coach, you may need to step into the process earlier and more often than you are used to in therapy. Having said that, I realize that many therapists are proactive but for now, I am talking to those of you who might not be. As a coach, you need to cut into an elaborate story and ask: 'Is this an area you want to focus on today?' or 'Out of all these issues, which would be most helpful to focus on today?' The aim is to enable clients to focus on the specific aspects of their life that they want to work on and not to leave them in storytelling mode. In this way, coaching approaches personal change differently from some therapeutic processes.

Avoiding goals and action planning

Goal-setting is a challenge for all novice coaches, and can be particularly so for therapists, who don't use it as a core element of their work. The section on goal-setting identified some of the issues for therapists, for example, that goal-setting and action planning can be unfamiliar processes. Coaching fails most when the goals are not specified. Change and learning cannot happen unless action is taken or behaviour altered. Arriving at the actions can be a challenge, as therapists sometimes concentrate on processing the clients' thoughts and feelings rather than bringing into focus the actions that need to be taken.

Holding more than the end time in mind

Coaching follows a more structured approach than do many therapies, with each session moving through a process related to the goals for the session. Your aim is to take the client through that process and to arrive at actions that will progress their goals. As the coach, you are managing that process. The time is structured to involve purposeful activity, aimed at goal-setting or achievement. As therapists, often the only times you have to attend to are when the session starts and ends. This is different, perhaps, for those of you who follow a particular framework within your sessions. Some therapists, moving into coaching, say that managing the time and process is something that can be challenging, as it represents a different way of working. They sometimes find that the session ends before they have moved the client from the core of the session through into the actions. When setting off in coaching, therefore, you might find you have to focus hard on holding that structure while at the same time being responsive to clients, and where they are in the work.

Novice coaches sometimes worry, too, about how they will fill a two-hour session. When they get started though, they usually find the time is fully used. For a therapist moving from 50- or 60-minute sessions, this may also require some personal re-orientation as you change your internal clock to a setting for shorter session times.

Thinking for the client

There is a tendency for therapists to think for the client. That is, they often think they need more information about clients' situations and internal experience before they can make an intervention. This can lead them to ask a range of information-seeking questions or to want to enrich the emerging picture. In doing this, they are not moving the client on. Sometimes gathering information will be necessary, but therapists need to let go of the belief that they need a full picture before they can work with the clients' issues.

Many therapists are used to thinking for their clients. That is, bringing analytical skills to bear and deciding how to progress the work. They are less used to asking clients or checking with them. The easiest way to find out if something has been helpful or not is to ask the client. As a coach, you don't have to work it out by yourself. Novice coaches can also be anxious that something difficult might occur in a session and that the client might not be able to cope until the next session. You can ask clients: 'Is there anything that you would like from me before we meet next?' If they think a telephone or email conversation would be helpful, they will tell you. If you find you are making assumptions about what the client needs, or doesn't need, ask them so that you are not going off at a tangent. Remember, clients know what they need. They don't need you to work that out for them.

Getting stuck in a helping/healing orientation

This is closely linked to thinking for the client. If you get stuck in a therapy orientation of healing or reparation, you will not be coaching. If you start to feel concerned about the client's well-being and respond from an over-nurturing parent ego-state, you are not coaching. As the coach, you need to focus on staying with a process mindset. If you have concerns, check them out with clients and find out if they think they have something they want to change or address. Stay in coaching mode.

Using therapy-speak and a lot of empathetic stroking

Empathy is an important aspect of coaching and clients need to feel that the coach understands their situation and feelings. However, therapists becoming coaches often respond to the client with a lot of calming restatements or repetitions of what the client is saying. This often results in an expansion of the client's description of the situation, which can be at the expense of moving forward. It is a judgement that coaches make about how long to keep encouraging clients to talk about their situation and when that is preventing the coaching process being enacted. There are no hard and fast rules, but it is something that you may want to watch for as you start coaching.

There are certain responses therapists have developed in their work with therapy clients. This cannot be generalized but there are phrases and language that non-therapists identify as therapy-speak. This is often how therapists frame up an intervention, in the use of particular phrasing which are part of your therapy practice, in your tone of voice or body language. Often we are deaf to it and our therapy clients get used to it too and may even start using the same language themselves. Mostly it occurs when the coach is falling away from the coaching orientation and feeling themselves more to be in the therapy role. In coaching, clients tend to react to therapy-speak since it is not what they are expecting and it sounds alien to them. Be aware as you begin to coach how much you are holding on to your therapeutic orientation and how that might be impacting on your clients.

Worrying about how everything can be addressed within a time limited coaching contract

Some coaching contracts may be limited to up to three sessions. Therapists moving into coaching can find this challenging if they are used to working with people over an extended period. It is less likely to be an issue for you if you are familiar and comfortable with working in a time limited way, for example, in a GP practice or where the number of sessions is limited owing to resource constraints. If that is not your experience, you may worry about how you will work with all the issues you have identified. If this is happening, you are still in therapist mode and need to shift yourself into a coaching orientation. In coaching, the responsibility is with the clients as to how they want to use the time, and where their focus should be. Clients have entered into a contract and are well aware of how long they have. It is important that you enable them to use the time in as focused a way as possible so that the maximum amount of personal change can be achieved. In a three session contract, you and the client are able to map the current context, clarify goals, and set out an action plan for achieving them. The client's role is to continue that work with the support of other people. You can do useful work within three sessions. Working over more sessions may enable the client to achieve more goals and to have the support during the implementation process.

Asking the why questions and going after the developmental psychology or internalized experience

You will, I hope, by this stage in the book have a sense of the future-focus of coaching and that you don't need to know about causal factors to bring about change to thoughts and beliefs. Therapists moving into coaching can struggle at first to stop themselves asking the why questions, for example, when you ask questions that are intended to give an answer to the thought: 'How did this come to be like this for you?' or when you are following a hunch that there might be something to explore or bring to light within the clients psycho-emotional experience: 'Tell me all about what you are experiencing.'

There are times in coaching when clients make a link between past and

BARRIERS, PROBLEMS AND CHALLENGES

present experience and find this insightful, just as clients do in therapy. This often happens when working with self-limiting beliefs that have resulted from developmental experience. Clients may recall school or family experiences and realize, often for the first time, that there is a connection with the present. This differs from some therapies, in that it comes from the client, out of the coaching process, not from the coach leading the client to the past.

There are also times, including at the beginning of a coaching relationship, when you need to find out about clients' history and the main events in their life. The past isn't forbidden territory in coaching, it is just that it is brought into the work far less often than in many therapies.

As a coaching therapist, you are likely to meet temptations to look into the past or to explore the full range of the client's internal experience. For example, you may work with a client who is finding it difficult to identify what she wants for herself. In her explorations she may refer often to her father and his view of her life so far. This might lead you to deduce that her options were limited by her need of his approval. If this were a therapy session, you might encourage her to tell you about him and her relationship with him, to explore her feelings about the relationship and any memories that might be evoked.

As her coach, you might also feel that exploring this relationship might lead to healthier outcomes for her, and you wouldn't ignore your hunch, you would respond to it differently. Staying within a coaching orientation gives you some choices about what you might suggest to her to open up what is becoming an impasse. The starting point would be to ask her if she wishes to change anything in the relationship with her father; in that way you are giving her the responsibility to decide what she wants to be different. You are then in the coaching process of goals, actions and moving into the future. As part of this, you could explore with her what ideas she has for how she might present her goals to her father and suggest that she practises through a two chair exercise.

If she says she doesn't want to change anything regarding her relationship with her father, that is her choice. If she is stuck in an either/or situation you would suggest working on that, to expand the range of possibilities and challenging any self-limiting beliefs that she wants to change. For example, she might have a belief that she can either stay in banking and win her father's approval, or she can go to art college and lose it, neither of which being what she wants.

Your heightened sensitivity to the links between the present and the client's possible psycho-emotional experience is a rich resource you bring to coaching. You may, for example, feel more confident in asking clients if they wish to change anything in a complex relationship or in their relationship with the world or the future. You may be more attuned than coaches without your background and expertise, to some of the client's psycho-emotional infrastructure. As a coach however, the decision about whether to change elements of these relationships is with the clients and not you. The coaching orientation to this change process is that of moving to the future, through what would they like to be different, and not through: 'How did it get like this?' or 'What is this like for you?' type interventions.

You may also be more likely to identify factors within the client's psychological make up that may be less amenable to a coaching approach. For example, you may work with clients who you sense may benefit from a process that will allow them to accommodate past experience or to establish a more secure internal base for themselves. The coaching response would be as before, that is, to ask if that is something they want to do some work on. The difference in this scenario is that it would not be you that takes them into that work. As the coach, you would work with them to identify how they might want to do that and to offer some names of therapists.

Working with emotions

Coaching involves feelings. Its cognitive-behavioural orientation works by linking feelings to thoughts. That is, by checking the feelings associated with a thought, in particular to identify if new thoughts create positive feelings. A trap for some novice coaches who are therapists, is that they want to explore the client's emotional life and experience and to encourage the expression of disavowed feelings. Such feelings may well arise in relation to self-limiting beliefs or in talking about goals: for example, feelings about being sent away to school, or having been bullied or feeling scared beneath a brave front. In this case the exercises may provide clients with insight, something they might wish to work on within a coaching or therapeutic frame. If they choose to work within the coaching frame, you would take them through the coaching process in the same way as for any other aspect of their life they wish to change. The difference is that you do not take up the therapy orientation and work with the clients' feelings as you would as a therapist.

As a coach, though, you need to give space to feelings and their expression. For example, a client might come to a session having had some bad news and in telling you, feelings well up. You may invite the client to talk about the feelings as well as to give space to their expression. However, you would hold in mind the need to clarify goals for the session and would find a suitable space to ask something like: 'This news has had a big impact on you and I wonder whether you want to use this session to work on what has happened or whether there are other things that you want to get from today?' The coaching frame starts with what clients want to focus on. If they say they want to work on what has happened, as the coach you wouldn't suggest they stay with their feelings or make connections with other experiences. For example, perhaps a client has been badly affected after receiving some negative feedback. In a therapy mode you might encourage the use of feeling responses to make connections with developmental experience fully to express all the feelings that have been generated. As a coach, you would take a different tack and could suggest using a guided imagery exercise. This could provide some emotional protection and distance, making it easier to reflect on the choice of response, including which elements of the feedback to accept. In this way, you are acknowledging the feelings and working with the client to a resolution or learning from which personal change can result. In using such exercises you are also giving clients a process they can use for themselves should a similar situation happen to them again. You are also reminding them that they have choices about how they respond.

As the coach, your response would depend on the cause of the emotional disturbance in the present. Whatever you do, you would stay in the present and move the client into the future. You may decide to ask the client: 'What would be most helpful to you right now?' or 'How would you like us to work with this emotion and the experience?' In this way you are respecting the adult:adult nature of the relationship and are not falling into the expert role of knowing what the client needs to work on.

Failing to use a range of coaching techniques

Coaching uses a range of techniques which are often new to novice coaches, even those coming from a therapy background. You will need to avoid the trap of staying in your comfort zone in favour of developing your confidence to use the full range of coaching interventions. For example, as a coach, you may avoid giving clients feedback about their behaviour. The use of feedback in coaching is on those aspects of behaviour that the client can change (see Chapter 6). If this is not something that, as a novice coach, you are used to doing, you may avoid it as a technique. Similarly, if you are not used to using guided imagery or exercises involving the imagination, and don't develop your skills in using them, you may never incorporate them into your coaching repertoire. To be a coach you need to use all your therapy skills within a coaching orientation *and* use the full range of coaching techniques.

When to suggest the client sees another practitioner

As a coach you wouldn't refer clients to another practitioner. However, you might identify with them that they may be able to benefit from a different process. You might also give them the names of people you feel it may be useful for them to contact.

Deeper psycho-emotional issues

The issue for novice non-therapist coaches can be the failure to recognize that clients have deeper psycho-emotional problems than they, or coaching, can really work with. People with psycho-emotional needs, for example, as a result of developmental disturbance or trauma, are less likely to be able to take up the sense of agency needed for coaching. They may not have sufficient capacity for mentalization, that is, the ability to reflect objectively on their situation. It might also be that in order to survive, they have learnt to develop their will power and that is over riding their sense of agency. As a consequence, they may have lost touch with what is meaningful and important to their inner well-being.

This is an area that coaches without a therapeutic background have to learn about. As a therapist, you are likely to be able to identify these problems sooner. You may also be able to work, as a coach, with people who are carrying levels of emotional disturbance in a way that would take non-therapist coaches out of their depth. In so doing, you may be able to enable them to take up a greater capacity for moving into the future and for taking action. However, it is important that you stay within a coaching framework and do not slip into therapy mode. If clients need therapy, including cognitive-behavioural therapy, or are not going to benefit from coaching, that needs to be discussed with them so that they can take action to get the help they need.

Different expertise

It might be that clients need some particular advice or input from someone with specialist knowledge or training. For example, they may need to see a financial adviser, or a debt management adviser or an image consultant. Getting help to take forward their goals will be part of their action plan. As the coach, you may find it helpful to develop contacts with people offering these services so that you can pass on their names, and perhaps get referrals back from them. Who the client contacts is their choice, and you should give them more than one name to follow up.

When it doesn't seem to be working

Sometimes the chemistry just doesn't work between client and coach. If you become aware of that feeling and there is something you can do to change it, do so. If your values are challenged and you feel compromised, or if rapport and working alliance are hard to establish and maintain, face up to it: it's not working. The best thing is for you and the clients to talk about it so that they have the opportunity to choose if they would rather work with someone else. If you feel you can't begin or continue working with a client, be honest. You may choose to talk it through in supervision and if that doesn't change anything, find a way of presenting the problem to the client in a way that is respectful and is mediated by your adult ego-state. Provide some names of your coaching colleagues who you feel might be able to work effectively with the client. Let both of you move on.

10 Which coaching market?

Most coaches work in private practice or as employees of a coaching or organizational consultancy. Some may work as employees within an organization with coaching as part of their work, for example, members of staff counselling services or education and training services.

Of the potential markets for private practice, life coaching – that is, seeing self-referred and self-paying clients – is the closest to a private therapy practice. While the orientation is different, coaching marketing and practice management have many similarities to running a therapy practice.

The most different, for many therapists, is the business coaching market. That is coaching managers and others within organizations, where their performance and career may be the focus of their goals and actions. It is often this market that is attractive to therapists as it provides a new direction and a potentially higher fee rate.

If you are thinking of moving into coaching to increase your fee level, you need to take certain factors into account. As a coach, you have marketing options that may not feel as open to you within therapy. For example, you might decide to market your services to people on high incomes so that you can charge a higher fee. If you charge more, you need to be able to meet clients' expectations around that fee; they are likely to want to feel the impact of the coaching from the beginning. They may also have expectations about the surroundings or location in which they meet you. It is possible that some therapy clients are aware that their therapists are on a low income and accept surroundings that aren't that favourable to them.

You also have to think through, having decided on your market, what you are going to call yourself. While there is some gradual understanding among the public about what a life coach does, those using this title can practice in different ways. Non-directive coaches use the title, as do those who use a directive coaching model. You will need, therefore, to make your approach clear in your marketing material and contracting.

If you are going to work in businesses, using the title Executive Coach implies that you are sufficiently experienced to work with the most senior people in companies. If this doesn't represent your level of expertise, you could call yourself a performance coach or development coach.

Table 10.1 draws together the similarities and differences of these two broad markets and the decisions you may need to make.

Table 10.1 Differences between personal/life coaching and business coaching

	Personal/Life Coaching	*Business Coaching*
Referrals	Self-referral	Self-referral or third party referral
Who pays	The client	The employer
Coaching package choices	Telephone coaching and/or face-to-face	Face-to-face more common, mixed with telephone coaching.
Number, length and spread of sessions	Telephone coaching: 30- or 45-minutes fortnightly or three weekly after initial longer session. Perhaps for up to 2 or more months. Could be on-going. Face-to-face: Packages of 4–6 × one and a half or two-hour sessions, every 4 weeks. If one-hour sessions, first session usual two-hours. Package repeated if valuable	Face-to-face: Often 2, 3 or 4 × two-hour session packages, spread over 3–5 months, repeated if beneficial
Payment	Per session, per package in advance or monthly	Per session, per package in advance or monthly
Venue	Coach's consulting room	Coach's consulting room or in an arranged venue
Who travels?	The client	The coach might decide to travel to the clients. Clients might travel to the coach, depending on distances involved
Focus of work	Holistic, so would include work-related goals	Holistic, likely to have work performance and career goals
Fee issues	If telephone coaching, client calls the coach so pays for the telephone call	If coach travelling to client, may decide to charge travelling costs and for travelling time
Marketing issues	Do you want to aim at people with higher or lower incomes? What fee income do you want to generate?	Which businesses has your background best prepared you for?
Coach employment	In private practice	In private practice or employed by coaching provider
Titles used	Life Coach, Personal Coach, Gestalt Coach (if gestalt trained)	Performance coach, executive coach, management coach, career coach, development coach

The business coaching market

If you want to work in the business market, however, there are some factors that you may need to address. Coaching has been an established part of leadership and management development for several years. There is a growing body of evidence attesting to the effectiveness of coaching in improving and enhancing performance. Organizations also use coaching to support staff through career progression and transition, for example, which results from organizational restructuring.

This market will require specific things from you as a coach. You would be working with businesses, with the aim of enabling your clients to enhance, or improve their performance. The sponsor needs to see the impact of the coaching process on the individual. There is, therefore, an additional level of assessment of the impact of the coaching process.

Some therapists may have values that are in conflict with those of business, or of some businesses. Businesses embody a different culture than most therapy organizations. With certain exceptions, they tend to pay little attention to the management and processing of feelings, tend to move quickly and change is continual. You will need to feel comfortable working within this culture to be an effective coach. That doesn't mean that you have to like or accept all aspects of it; indeed, you may raise organizational development issues with those who hire you. You do, however, have to feel sufficiently comfortable working in it. There may be some businesses that you decide not to work in, for example, you may disagree with what they produce or their way of operating. That is your choice.

The holistic nature of coaching remains in these settings. For example, clients may want to make changes to their non-work life which would give them renewed energy or take away other stress factors to enable them to engage differently with their work. Sometimes clients may only talk about non-work changes. However, in this setting, you both know that the purpose of coaching is to enable their personal, managerial and leadership development.

Organizations use coaching to help their managers develop their effectiveness: this may include dealing with other people and managing their own work. It is often especially helpful to clients new into a job, or those taking on new responsibilities or challenges. They may want to review their career and think about what their next steps are. Sometimes clients use coaching to make changes to their levels of confidence and personal presence, so that they can increase the extent to which they can influence others. Coaching is also sometimes used to help people who are under-performing, with the implicit or explicit expectation that the individual will improve as a result of the coaching.

Businesses can create conditions that drive individuals to an unhealthy work/life balance. For this reason, coaching sometimes results in the individual considering a career or job change. Most organizations accept this and would rather not have employees who can't deal with the pressures and demands placed on them. Sometimes, it is the clients' strategies and systems that cause them to have difficulties managing the work expectations. These can be changed through coaching, enabling them to be more effective and less stressed.

To operate in this environment you need well-honed coaching competences, and in addition, a range of other capabilities. For example, you must have credibility in the business world, or the part of the business world in which you propose to work. This means you have to understand about business leadership and management and to appreciate organizational dynamics. You need to be able to talk about the business issues with the sponsor and to bring your understanding as a resource to working with the client. You can't be naïve about business or the pressures and demands on leaders. To be an effective coach with business managers you must understand enough about the climate in which they work. You don't need to be fluent in the specifics, but you have to understand the dynamics of leadership and management, about power and authority, and the market pressures that bear on a specific business. Coaching at this level also includes an element of training on issues that people most often bring to coaching. These include, for example, delegation, influencing, managing upwards and dealing with difficult people. You would need to be able to offer the client some frameworks and exercises that help them work through some of these dynamics. For example, you might tell a client about the Transactional Analysis ego-states and invite them to apply these to the situation they are considering.

Trust is equally important as within therapy relationships. However, in organizational coaching, those commissioning your services need to be able to trust that you will keep their commercial information confidential. As the coach, you will hear about a company's fortunes or misfortunes, much of the latter will not be in the public domain. You may also be coaching people who have a public profile and who have an image to protect. This doesn't change any of the rules about confidentiality that you will be familiar with from your therapeutic practice, but it places them in a different context.

You also need to look the part, that is, present yourself in an attire appropriate to the business setting. This may be more or less formal depending on the culture of the business. This means business suits, where they are the norm, and a different approach to personal presentation than is necessary for most therapy settings. The key factor is not to present yourself as the stereotypical therapist if you want to be taken seriously as an organizational coach. The stereotype of a therapist, from an organizational perspective, is that of someone in informal dress (flowing skirts and dangling earrings for women, sandals and open-neck shirts for men), who are not organized and who want people to get in touch with their feelings or spirituality all the time. The stereotype of business, possibly held by therapists, might be that they are financially driven, money-grabbing and do not pay enough attention to people's feelings, relationships or spirituality. Neither stereotype is accurate, but like all prejudices they often contain a grain of truth. Some businesses may conform to this stereotype, many don't. Many are aware of the emotional, relational and spiritual aspects of human experience and want to support their staff in becoming effective and fulfilled.

Finally, you have to be able to feel like an equal to senior people in organizations, who often carry a considerable amount of role power and authority. It won't work if you fall into a 'child ego-state' or want to challenge the power within their role. You need to be able to feel the same size, psychologically, as those with whom you are working. Therapists tend not to have to confront this in their therapy practice; often others, particularly clients, may see you as the one with the power.

It may be that you already have some business-related experience. In this case, it would be easier to become a coach in that aspect of business rather than to go into totally new organizational settings. For example, if you have been a teacher at some time, coaching in schools may be a good starting point. Alternatively, if you are an NHS therapist or health care worker, you may find coaching within the health sector is a viable option as you will carry credibility with potential clients, and will understand the nature of the healthcare sector. To develop these organizational coaching qualities you may need to attend some additional development workshops or courses to augment your abilities in these areas. It is important that you read the books that explore these issues. The Bibliography is useful for suggesting further reading.

These organizational requirements can be new and challenging to therapists. You may feel organizational coaching would pull you too far out of your comfort zone. It certainly challenges the model of doing charitable work that is often associated with some approaches to therapy. Perhaps you chose to work in therapy to get away from some of these issues and demands; or to achieve a particular life style. However, if you can fulfil the expectations of businesses, and can operate within that culture, you will be able to access, potentially, a more lucrative practice. Fees within organizational coaching tend to be considerably more than for life coaching or therapy. They are more akin to consultancy fees, on which they are often based. Coaching is valued within business and employers are prepared to pay a market rate for that level of expertise. The fact that it is valued in that way means coaches need to be able to deliver against high professional expectations.

If you aim to coach those at the top of businesses or organizations, you would call yourself an executive or leadership coach. If that is too much of a stretch for you, because of limited business experience, you might decide to focus your marketing on the middle management or supervisory level. You might call yourself a performance, management or leadership coach. Those you coach would be people who head up teams or smaller units of the organization's work. You would still need to understand organizational politics and dynamics, group processes and the issues facing that level of management. The fee level would be lower than for executive coaching, but still higher than for therapy. Such an approach might provide a more feasible entry point to working in organizations. From there you could build up your reputation and your client base.

Confidentiality in organizational coaching

Confidentiality, when it comes to organizational coaching, can be more complicated as you, in effect, have two clients, the sponsor and the actual client. Imagine the scene: a company director, Bill in a phone call to Judith, the coach:

BILL: Judith, I'd like you to coach Anne as she is not developing as quickly as I need her to and is making a few enemies.

JUDITH: Thanks for thinking of me Bill; I'm happy in principle to work with Anne but she needs to feel OK about my being her coach and after an exploratory session, she needs to feel free to say if she doesn't think working with me would be useful. Would that be OK?

BILL: Yes, that's fine.

JUDITH: Also, Bill, you know that I can't tell you what is said in the coaching sessions as they are confidential. I realize you will need some information about what is happening but is it OK for us to agree you will talk to Anne directly about what she is getting as a result of the coaching?

BILL: Yes, that's fine. Let's agree four sessions and see how it goes. I'll send you a copy of her performance objectives so you can see what I need her to be doing at work.

The coaching starts. At the first session Judith checks boundaries with Anne and explains that what is said is confidential, that yes, Judith does know Bill but that whatever Anne tells her will be confidential. Judith also tells Anne that Bill sent her a copy of her performance objectives and asks her about them. In the second session, Anne says she finds Bill unacceptably bullying and that she feels he is putting a lot of pressure on her. She also says that the relationship is so bad that he doesn't really talk to her any more and so she isn't sure what he wants from her.

Judith's heart sinks. Has Bill set her up to talk with Anne so that he won't have to? Has he set her up so he can say: 'We tried coaching and that didn't work either, so sorry, Anne, but this is the end of the road?' Is Anne using her to get back at Bill? Is Bill a bully; is he part of the problem? What should Judith do? As Anne is giving her the information, Judith has to keep it confidential. However, she might go back to Bill to clarify his goals for the coaching and do what she can to ensure that he articulates these to Anne.

Or two sessions pass, Anne engages with the coaching. The phone goes. It's Bill:

BILL: Judith. Hi, just wanted to talk to you about how things are going with Anne. We are still having problems with her you know, she just isn't making the grade. I just wondered if there was anything you wanted to tell me?

What should Judith do? She should refer to the contract she set up with Bill around sharing of information. If she spelt this out properly at the beginning she would be able to respond:

JUDITH: Bill, I'm sorry to hear you are still having problems. You'll remember when we set up my work with Anne, I said I wouldn't be able to share any information with you. If you have concerns about Anne, you need to be talking to her so that she can do something about them. I can work with her on what she decides to do.

Suppose this scenario had happened during the initial set up call:

BILL: Judith, I've got a real problem here that I need you to help me sort out. Anne just isn't making it and is driving everyone mad, she just isn't delivering. I wondered if you would coach her over the next six months to help see if she can make the grade?
JUDITH: Bill, thanks for thinking of me. Sounds as if you have a problem. Have you talked to Anne about the issues? Does she know from you the problems you see?
BILL: Well, not really. I've hinted but she doesn't really take the hint.
JUDITH: Hm ... Bill, I'm not comfortable knowing something about Anne that she doesn't know, I wonder how we could overcome that?
BILL: To tell you the truth, I just don't know how to put it to her.
JUDITH: Bill, would it be helpful for us to have a coaching session to help you tell Anne these things and to deal with her apparent underperformance?

This happens. Judith then sees Anne.

> JUDITH: Anne, you will know that Bill has asked me to be your coach, but I have told him that I am only happy to do that if you want to work with me. So at the end of this session we need to talk about that. It's important that you feel confident in our working together. You also know that Bill has shared some things about how he perceives your work, I wonder if you could tell me what he has told you?

Anne tells Judith that he has told her she isn't developing into the role quickly enough and that he is offering her this opportunity of coaching to help her development.

> JUDITH: Yes, that is the information he gave me. I wondered how you felt about what he said.
>
> ANNE: I feel frustrated as I am doing my best but I feel he isn't giving me a chance.

As the coach, you would work with Anne and help her manage upwards and create a different working relationship with Bill if that is one of her goals. If her goal was to change jobs, you'd work with her on that.

Providing coaching to an organization, therefore, can bring dilemmas that need to be resolved. Some of the principles are:

- The coach is there for the client who is receiving the coaching. The coach isn't part of the organization's performance management system and doesn't carry a responsibility to make sure the client improves his or her performance.
- Where there is a performance issue, the coach and client may consider how to get more feedback about the client's performance so there is some data to work with; or together they might work with established role competences so the clients can assess him/herself. This enables the client to take some control over the analysis that is being made and decide what he or she wants to do about it.
- Using personality and other psychometric instruments can aid self-development and help clients better understand communication breakdowns or differences within work teams and other relationships.
- The coach cannot share any information about the client's work with a third party. It's up to the client to discuss the coaching with the boss and this should be part of the contractual expectations.
- The coach should try not to have information about clients that hasn't been shared with them. This is not always possible and the

coach has to be able to manage the confidentiality boundaries while also working fully in the service of the clients.
- Sometimes it might be the boss who may benefit most from the coaching. A coach should avoid coaching both boss and member of staff, as it's too easy to get caught in the middle.
- Internal coaches have to be experts in keeping the coaching confidential. They may be coaching staff that they also work with in different contexts and may end up with a lot of information about a lot of people. This might generate ethical dilemmas and supervision will be important to help work these through.

Contracting and organizational coaching

As you will realize, contracting for organizational coaching often involves two other people, the sponsor and the client, Bill and Anne in the example given above. You need to get the contract clear with both parties. In doing this, it is useful to think about the contracting triangle, originally described by Julie Hay in her book *TA for Trainers* (1992).

The contracting triangle is shown in figure 10.1 and involves Bill, Anne and Judith. Bill is the sponsor, that is, he is allocating funds to Anne's coaching and has expectations of how he wants Anne to use the coaching. He needs to make this clear directly to Anne, and not use Judith as his proxy communicator. In effect, Bill has an informal contract with Anne. Judith and Bill have a contract that sets out the number of sessions, costs, and the boundaries to confidentiality. Judith would also use the contract to explain the principles of coaching, just as she would with an individual client. Judith and Anne have a contract, again setting out the principles and practice of coaching, the role of the coach, and how confidentiality will be handled. Coaching clients have to be willing partners in the work. If they are not, it would be unwise to work with them. You are not there to be a surrogate manager; you are there to focus on the clients' concerns in just the same way as any coaching relationship.

Bill, the boss, who is sponsoring the coaching

Judith, the coach   *Anne*, the client

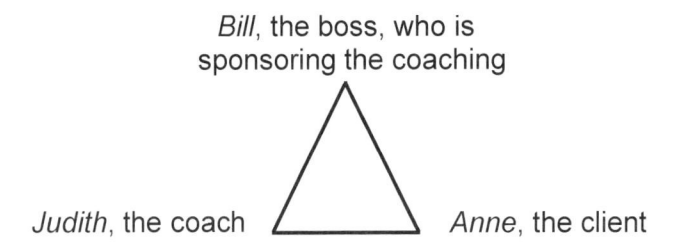

Figure 10.1 The contracting triangle

Use of personality and other instruments

If you coach in an organization, you will find it useful to be able to use a range of psychometric and assessment instruments. These might include self-assessment or peer assessment instruments and personality or personal quality questionnaires. These provide feedback for clients and help enhance their self-awareness and understanding. Such instruments can add a valuable dimension to mapping the 'now' and the resources available within clients and can throw light on things that they might find difficult or stressful. There are many such products on the market. In most cases you will have to attend a preparation workshop and be a licensed practitioner in the use of the specific instrument. Peer review processes are sometimes used in organizations, for example 360-degree feedback questionnaires. These enable clients to identify up to 12 or 15 people whom they ask to complete the questionnaire anonymously. They then return them to a third party who synthesizes the responses and creates a client report. The people asked will be peers, staff who report to the client, and those to whom the client reports. These processes are not without their problems and need to be used with caution, particularly in organizations where people are not used to giving and receiving feedback in this way. For example, clients can be devastated by negative feedback that has never been said to them face-to-face. As the coach, you need to have well-developed skills in helping clients understand what the feedback is telling them and in enabling them to work through what their responses are going to be.

Running a mixed practice of therapy and coaching

Perhaps your goal is to have a mixed practice of therapy and coaching. If so, there are a few things to consider. For example, if someone rings up and asks for an appointment but isn't specific about whether they want therapy or coaching, how will you handle them? Mostly clients are specific about the process they want to access. But if they are not, you would talk them through the coaching and therapy processes either on the phone or through a 45-minute 'look-see' meeting. Running a life coaching practice alongside a therapy practice might result in confusion for the clients unless you are clearly able to set out the differences. It would be important to be clear about the different approaches, what they offer, and the situations they are best placed to help. For example, you may state to the client and in your marketing information that if someone is looking for help for an eating disorder, the emotional consequences of traumatic experience or suffering from emotional disturbances such as bereavement or depression, they may be helped better through a therapeutic orientation. People who feel stuck or want to make changes in their life and relationships, who are in transition, or feel life is not giving them what they want and feel unfulfilled, may be better helped by coaching.

Might you be marketing coaching and therapy in competition with each other? This is a possibility, although you would be differentiating between the two and in effect appealing to two different markets. However there may be problems in having two different fee rates. This would need to be explained in a way that the client does not feel one is more valuable than the other or that they have to choose the cheapest or the more expensive process. This can be done as coaching tends to be a shorter-term process, with longer sessions.

Would you refer a client from one part of your practice, for example therapy, to coaching, or vice versa? Once you and the client agree a way of working, it is important to keep to that contract and respect the boundaries of the practice. The work shouldn't shift from coaching to therapy or vice versa mid-way through. That is not to say that you wouldn't use coaching approaches at times in your therapy work, or aspects of therapy within your coaching work but you wouldn't switch from one frame to another. If clients identify that therapy might be what they need rather than coaching, you would coach them through that thinking towards a decision, including who they might work with. Similarly, if in therapy or counselling the client started thinking of getting coaching instead, you would work with that within the framework of your orientation. It is my view, that it is inappropriate to refer a client to yourself, that is to refer a coaching client who wants therapy to your therapy practice. This would raise issues about boundaries and the relationship. If you work in a practice with other coaches or therapists, then those issues don't arise and the client is free to choose to work within a different orientation with one of your colleagues or with someone else.

If your coaching work is primarily through companies, then the difference with your therapy work is more clearly delineated as is your marketing and fee structure.

11 Integrating coaching with other practises

I have been talking about coaching as a discrete activity between a coach and a client. However, there are many ways in which coaching techniques can contribute to therapy and make a useful addition to our interpersonal skills, for example, in how we relate to colleagues, friends and our children.

Coaching is not therapy; it is a different process. Having said that, many of the approaches within coaching exist within solutions-focused and other similar orientations to therapy. There may, therefore, be opportunities for bringing the two together in a dynamic and creative way by those who bestride both practices. It is possible both to look forward into the future and downwards into the psycho-emotional life of the client. Perhaps it doesn't have to be either/or. At the moment there is no term or established framework for such a synthesized practice, other than bringing the names together such as gestalt, psycho-dynamic, or relational coaching. It may be that such a synthesis could diminish the impact of both aspects of the practice, ending up as poor coaching and poor therapy. Alternatively it could be that the combination is a rich and progressive one for the client.

Coaching approaches can be used within therapies and counselling, as can the framework for personal change embedded within the coaching process. Many therapists already use some of these approaches in their work and haven't labelled them coaching. For example, at the beginning of therapy or counselling it can be helpful to be goal-orientated:

HARRY (therapist/counsellor): Susan, you have come into counselling because you are crying a lot and feeling really down, I'm wondering what it is you hope to get out of this counselling process.
SUSAN: Well, I want to feel better.
HARRY: Has there been a time in your life when you felt better in the way you are hoping for out of this process?
SUSAN: Well, it's hard to think of one, but I suppose I want to feel more like I did five years ago before all this started.
HARRY: Tell me what you were experiencing five years ago, how were you behaving, what was going on in your life?

From there Harry can work with Susan to frame up some goals around what feeling better really means, while at the same time enabling Susan to develop some vision for things being different. This also gives them an ending point, something to refer to as the work progresses within whichever orientation Harry is using.

Another integration is the use of the *miracle question* associated with solutions-focused work: 'Imagine that when you wake up in the morning your problem has totally disappeared, how will you spend the day?' These are practises that many therapists already use.

Coaching approaches can also be relevant to enable someone to enter into therapy or counselling:

HARRY: Dave, I'm hearing that you feel overwhelmed by so many things at the moment. I wonder if it would be helpful to do what we can to get a grip on some of those things before we delve deeper into your experience and feelings.

DAVE: I don't know, it just feels as if I have so many things pressing for my attention I am not sure how I am going to be able to do therapy anyway.

HARRY: If there was something we could do to make that more possible for you, what would be the best place to start?

DAVE: Well, I suppose I have to do something about the debts that I have run up as that is so hanging on my mind and I feel I can't do anything until that is sorted, but at the same time I just don't seem to be able to do anything about it.

HARRY: How would it be if we just focused on that for the moment, knowing that we will be practical in the short-term and then come back to working with what things are really like for you inside?

With Dave's agreement, they continue in coaching mode, so that Dave takes away an action to make an appointment with CAB to talk about managing his debts.

Another example of using a coaching approach could be by enabling someone to move into therapy but who is unable to see how she could find the time:

HARRY: Hazel, you have said that you feel that engaging with psychotherapy is what you want to be doing as you have this sense that there are some things that go way back and are quite deep within you affecting how you relate to others, but that at the moment you are just too busy to make the time. I'm wondering if you would like to do some work about how you could make that time available.

INTEGRATING COACHING WITH OTHER PRACTISES   **137**

Harry could have interpreted Hazel's inability to find the time as resistance to the work, but he holds back on articulating that until they have a psychotherapy contract in place. In taking a coaching approach he is not ignoring that as a possibility (within his orientation of working) but reserves judgement on it until they have agreed a contract.

Coaching approaches can also have a place towards the end of a therapy process when client and counsellor/therapist are preparing for the ending or are coming to a point when looking outwards and forwards again is important:

> JENNIFER: Lee, I wonder now what it is you want for yourself over the next three years? What do you hope will be happening for you then?

Or

> JENNIFER: Lee, it feels we have come a long way since we started and spent a lot of our time looking backwards and into your present relationships. I wonder what you see for yourself as you look forwards? If things go the way you hope, what will be happening for you in two–three years' time?

Jennifer may take that on through a coaching process, working in a less structured way than coaching but nonetheless taking Lee through visioning, goals, possibilities and actions.

There are also times within a therapy when using approaches associated with coaching enables some empowerment around an issue, which in turn enables some differently orientated work to follow.

> JANE (client): I am dreading this work meeting tomorrow with Lorna, I know I will find it hard to stand up to her.
> JAMES (therapist): If you were standing up to her, what would you do and say?
> JANE: Well, I'd tell her I didn't like the way she left early last week and I don't like her attitude towards Julie.
> JAMES: Can you imagine telling her that?
> JANE: Well, yes, I can actually, I don't know why it felt so difficult.
> JAMES: So how might you play the meeting tomorrow?

After Jane has responded, James can then take the focus back into other areas that will be less conscious and may be more connected with historical data:

> JAMES: I'm wondering, Jane, if this is also connected with what happens for you when you have to confront an older female colleague. What do you make of that?

This is a shift away from coaching and back into a different way of working. Another example of this might be:

SHARON: I hate it that I have nowhere to go when the others in the flat are watching television, stuff that I don't want to watch.
JAMES (deciding to use a coaching approach rather than, at this stage, exploring her experience and what gets evoked by it): You say you have nowhere to go, is there anywhere in the house that you could make into a place for you?
SHARON: Well, there's my room but it just doesn't feel comfortable; or there's the space at the top of the landing, it's like a little recess really.
JAMES: Which of these, if made comfortable, would feel best for you?
SHARON: Well, the top of the stairs recess really because then I am not shut away but I have some space for myself.
JAMES: So, is there anything you could do to that space which would make it a comfortable refuge for you?
SHARON: Yes, I could bring the chair from home (her parent's house) and put it there with a footstool and get a good lamp so I can read.
JAMES: So you could bring the chair, put in a footstool and lamp and that would feel like a good space for you? Can you imagine yourself in that space?
SHARON: Yes, I can, it would be really snug and I wouldn't feel so fed up with the others.
JAMES (moving to action): So what might you need to do first to make that happen?
SHARON: Well, I could get the chair next weekend when I am going home and probably pick up a light on the way home from the big hypermarket.
JAMES: So do you think you will do that?
SHARON: Yes, absolutely, I can't think why I haven't done that before. I feel so stupid.
JAMES (now going back to a therapeutic mode): Well, Sharon, I'm wondering what was going on for you when you felt there was no place for you in the sitting room.

Or

JAMES: I'm wondering what if felt like for you to feel shut out by the television and on your own.

James has shifted back to his therapy orientation and is inviting her to engage with her experience and feelings. He has, however, also enabled her to feel she has some power to move away from disabling feelings and take some action. He is honouring her experience, working with how she could change it *and* exploring what inner processes might have been evoked and what her emotional experience was.

There is also a place for acknowledgement and affirmation within therapy as many will testify from their own work. Therapists may well wish to acknowledge something in the client, for example: 'I'd like to acknowledge the courage you are summoning up to do this work' or encourage the client to do some self-affirming work, for example: 'I am lovable just as I am.' or 'I am valuable'. Many therapists will already use metaphor, guided imagery and imagination within their work. Those who don't may find a way to bring them more into their work so as to enable clients to imagine other states; to imagine something different from the either/or states that can be so prevalent in clients' thinking. In some ways, coaching challenges some therapies to reflect on how personal change is achieved, and the process that can best help that. Some therapies may be able to adopt more of a coaching approach to good effect than others. Some therapists may feel that it would be a dilution of the therapy and therefore inappropriate to add variations to the process.

Using coaching in work settings

There are many other opportunities and settings in which to use a coaching approach. For example, we train managers to use coaching techniques in their work as an interpersonal set of skills. In deploying these skills, they can empower their staff, enabling them to call on their own resourcefulness and creativity. This can have the impact of staff achieving increased job satisfaction and in being more effective. Using coaching in this way requires managers to shift away from a 'tell and direct' mode of working. This tell and direct approach, where staff are expected to do what their manager tells them can be prevalent in many organizations. It can bring short-term response but leads to a generalized disempowerment and dissatisfaction and is probably best kept for the times when only that approach would do. Managers may use some of the coaching exercises with groups. For example, a balance wheel can be applied to work priorities as a means of generating a discussion about how things are and what would be better. The basic balance wheel is a valuable exercise when used within coaching. For example:

> MANAGER: I wonder if it might be useful to identify all the priorities you are working on right now and pick out the top six, then see how satisfied you are with how they're going.

The group or individual identifies the key things being working on, and pick out the six. They then allocate them to the wheel, one for each section (figure 11.1).

140 THERAPIST INTO COACH

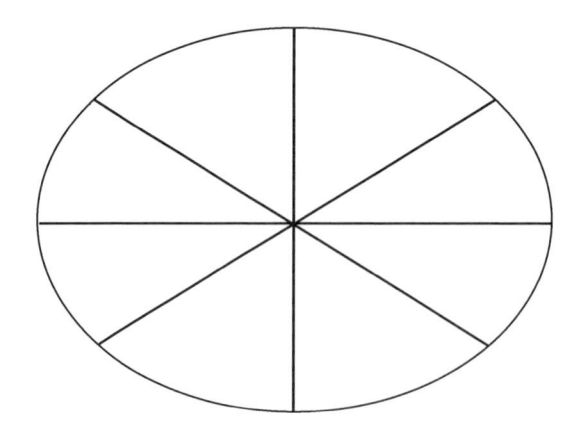

Figure 11.1 The balance wheel

> KAREN (the manager): Let's rate each for the level of satisfaction, with the centre being 0 and the outer rim being 10.

Having done that, a picture will emerge of some going well and others stagnating or not moving satisfactorily.

> KAREN: So, on which of these segments would it be most helpful to do some work first?

Having identified that:

> KAREN: Where would you like to be able to rate the level of satisfaction here in six months' time?

In this way she is inviting them to create a vision of a shift:

> KAREN: If you were already operating at that level of satisfaction, what would be happening differently, what might you and others be doing, saying or thinking?

Karen in coaching mode, continues to invite the team to create a clear vision of what improved satisfaction might look, feel and sound like.

> KAREN (pointing to one of the segments): I notice that on this segment here, you are rating your level of satisfaction high and I wondered if there was any learning there about what you or others did or didn't do that enabled this to be achieved.

In this way she is looking for the learning and seeing if there is any that can be effectively transferred. At no time is she looking to define or analyse the problem; she is not interested in the *why* but in what needs to be different to enable the group to feel a higher level of satisfaction. She will work with possibilities, enabling the team to create as many as possible. She might work with any self-limiting beliefs that arise and towards the end of the time for the discussion, be enquiring about action:

> Karen: So, what is the next step that needs to be taken here?

Karen might also apply coaching techniques on a one-to-one basis with members of her staff in more formalized coaching sessions, in short telephone or corridor conversations. We encourage managers to use powerful questions and purposeful enquiry as often as they can if they are really committed to enabling their staff and colleagues to develop their creativity and sense of empowerment.

I've included this example as you may also hold managerial or similar roles within your organization and I want to encourage you to use coaching approaches in that role as part of your full repertoire of skills.

Clients have also told me, and I know from my own experience, that these approaches can also be useful in interactions with our children. Rather than imposing a solution and going into the tell and direct mode, we can ask: 'What would you rather have?' or 'What would need to be different for you to feel school was important?' In this way we can further encourage our children to believe that they are resourceful and we can demonstrate our capacity to listen to them and work with them to find their own solutions.

Using powerful or enquiring questions, which aren't implied commands in a different form, can liberate something useful in you as well as in the person to whom the question is addressed within any meeting or forum. For example, simply asking: 'What would be most helpful to you?', to someone who was finding it difficult to take in some information, enables them to say: 'Well, I suppose I would find it more useful to see this demonstrated so I can get a sense of what it is.' That enables you to provide a developmental experience and to demonstrate that you are interested in what others need.

Every day will provide an opportunity for powerful questions, reframing, clarification and for a solutions, future and coaching focus. Similarly, there will be opportunities each week for goal exploration and setting, ideas-storming, and other processes to help ourselves and those around us respond to situations in which they find themselves. Coaching brings together many interpersonal skills that add value to all relationships.

End piece

I have tried to take you through the coaching process and to provide you with a sense of the language of coaching. Coaching is a motivating and empowering process, if done well. It can therefore help people to transform their lives. It isn't the best process for all; some people will benefit more from a therapeutic and spiritual process. That is how *they* will be enabled to transform their lives. There is enough room within the personal development and change field for coaching and for psychological therapies, in all their forms.

Coaching is an orientation and process that can be evaluated as it involves the setting of clear goals. There is a research base to turn to if that is your interest. Mostly the research studies have been carried out in organizational settings, as such contexts provide ready access to a cohort of 'coachees'. The European Mentoring and Coaching Council and many of the business schools are providing evidence about the practice of coaching that is encouraging and validating. Coaching in private practice shares similar problems with therapy when it comes to being able to carry out a sufficiently substantial evaluative project. However, you will know in your work with coaching clients whether the coaching is having the effect it should be having. Quite simply, is the client being able to move ahead with his or her goals?

Psychological therapists bring so much to coaching through their skills and knowledge of psychological processes. Coaching will be enriched by more therapists moving into the practice. As I have stated, coaching therapists need to stop doing some things and apply their skills in different ways to take up a coaching orientation.

However, they are starting from a solid foundation of practice and experience of the issues and boundaries of working on a one-to-one basis with clients.

I hope that this book has given you enough to get started on or has helped you decide that coaching maybe isn't for you. If it has encouraged you to develop your coaching practice, there are a number of books that will add to this one, particularly those in the same series and a range of training programmes, see the Bibliography.

Thank you for reading this book. If you have any comments or responses I would be pleased to hear them.

Julia Vaughan Smith
jvs@anaptys.co.uk

What next? Reflective exercise

Here are some questions to answer.

1. What are your goals in respect of coaching?
2. What challenges, if any, might setting up a private practice hold for you?
3. What challenges, if any, might working organizationally hold for you?
4. What additional development do you think you need to work as a coach in the way you are thinking?
5. How will you get sufficient practice, feedback and reflection to develop your learning?
6. Whose help do you need? (List as many names as you can think of.)
7. When you imagine yourself working as a coach, how and where are you working?

Bibliography

Amado, G. and Vansina, L. (2005) *The Transitional Approach in Action*. London: H. Karnac (Books) Ltd.
Argyris, C. (1992) *On Organisational Learning*. Oxford: Blackwell.
Bandler, R. and Grinder, J. (1979) *Frogs into Princes*. Utah, UT: Real People Press.
Beckhard, R. and Harris, R.T. (1987) *Organizational Transitions*. Reading, MA: Addison-Wesley Publishing.
Berne, E. (1964) *Games People Play*. London: Penguin.
Bridges, W. (1991) *Managing Transitions*. Reading, MA: Addison-Welsey.
Briggs Myers, I. and Myers, P. (1993) *Gifts Differing*. Palo Alto, CA: Consulting Psychologist Press Inc.
Carson, R. (1987) *Taming Your Gremlin: A Guide to Enjoying Yourself*. London: Harper and Row.
Cooperrider, D. and Whitney, D. (2005) *Appreciative Inquiry: A Positive Revolution in Change*. San Francisco, CA: Berrett-Koehler.
Covey, S. (1992) *The Seven Habits of Highly Effective People*. London: Simon and Schuster.
Elton Wilson, J. (1996) *Time-Conscious Psychological Therapy*. London: Routledge.
Follette, V., Ruzek, J. and Abueg, F.R. (1998) *Cognitive-Behavioural Therapies for Trauma*. London: The Guilford Press.
Garland, C. (ed.) (1998) *Understanding Trauma: A Psycholanalytical Approach*. 2nd edn. London: H. Karnac (Books) Ltd.
Golman, D. (1998) *Working with Emotional Intelligence*. London: Bloomsbury Publishing.
Gray, A. (1994) *An Introduction to the Therapeutic Frame*. London: Routledge.
Harris, T.A. (1973) *I'm OK – You're Okay*. London: Pan Books.
Hay, J. (1992) *Transactional Analysis for Trainers*. London: McGraw-Hill.
Hirschhorn, L. (1990) *The Workplace Within: Psychodynamics of Organizational Life*. London: The MIT Press.
Holmes, J. (2001) *The Search for the Secure Base*. Hove: Brunner-Routledge.
Honey, P. and Mumford, A. (1986) *The Manual of Learning Styles*. London: Peter Honey.
Huffington, C., Armstrong, D., Halton, W., Hoyle, L. and Pooley, J. (2004) *Working Below the Surface: The Emotional Life of Contemporary Organisations*. London: H. Karnac (Books) Ltd.
Hycner, R. and Jacobs, L. (1995) *The Healing Relationship in Gestalt Therapy*. Highland, NY: Gestalt Journal Press Inc.

Iles, V. (2006) *Really Managing Healthcare*. 2nd edn. Buckingham: Open University Press.
Jackson, C. (1996) *Understanding Psychological Testing*. Leicester: BPS Books.
Jones, J.E. and Bearley, W.L. (1996) *360-degree Feedback*. Valley Center, CA: Organizational Universe Systems.
Lago, C. and Thompson, J. (1996) *Race, Culture and Counselling*. Buckingham: Open University Press.
Lasch, C. (1979) *The Culture of Narcissism*. New York, NY: W.W. Norton & Company Inc.
McGruder Watkins, J. and Mohr, B. (2001) *Appreciative Inquiry: Change at Speed of Imagination*. San Francisco, CA: Jossey-Bass.
McLeod, J. (1997) *Narrative and Psychotherapy*. London: Sage Publications Ltd.
Mollon, P. (1993) *The Fragile Self*. London: Whurr Publishers Ltd.
Mollon, P. (2002) *Remembering Trauma*. London: Whurr Publishers Ltd.
Mullins, L. (1993) *Management and Organizational Behaviour*. London: Pitman Publishing.
Murdin, L. (2000) *How Much Is Enough?* London: Routledge.
Neenan, M. and Dryden, W. (2002) *Life Coaching: A Cognitive-Behavioural Approach*. London: Routledge.
Newton, J., Long, S. and Sievers, B. (2006) *Coaching in Depth: The Organizational Role Analysis Approach*. London: H. Karnac (Books) Ltd.
O'Conner, J. and Seymour J. (1990) *Introducing Neuro-Linguistic Programming*. London: Mandala.
O'Hanlan, B. (2003) *A Guide to Inclusive Therapy*. London: W.W. Norton & Company Ltd.
O'Hanlan, B. and Weiner-Davies, M. (2003) *In Search of Solutions: A New Direction in Psychotherapy*. London: W.W. Norton & Company Ltd.
O'Neill, M.B. (2000) *Executive Coaching with Backbone and Heart*. San Francisco, CA: Jossey-Bass.
Peltier, B. (2001) *The Psychology of Executive Coaching*. New York, NY: Brunner-Routledge.
Rogers, C.R. (1961) *On Becoming a Person*. London: Consultable.
Rogers, J. (2001) *Adults Learning*. 4th edn. Buckingham: Open University Press.
Rogers, J. (2004) *Coaching Skills, A Handbook*. Buckingham: Open University Press.
Schien, E.H. (2004) *Organizational Culture and Learning*. San Francisco, CA: Jossey-Bass.
Schulz, W. (1984) *The Truth Option*. Berkeley, CA: Ten Speed Press.
Schulz, W. (1989) *Profound Simplicity*. San Diego, CA: WSA Bantam.
Schwarz, R. (2002) *The Skilled Facilitator*. San Francisco, CA: Jossey-Bass.
Spoto, A. (1995) *Jung's Typology in Perspective*. Illinois, IL: Chiron Publications.
Stacy, R. (2001) *Complex Response Processes in Organizations: Learning and Knowledge Creation*. London: Routledge.
Starr, J. (2003) *The Coaching Manual*. London: Pearson Education Ltd.

Stewart, I. (1987) *TA Today. A New Introduction to Transactional Analysis*. Nottingham: Lifespace Publishing.

Strasser, F. and Strasser, A. (2001) *Existential Time-Limited Therapy*. Chichester: John Wiley & Sons, Ltd.

Williams, P. and Davis, D.C. (2002) *Therapist as Life Coach: Transforming your Practice*. New York, NY: W.W. Norton & Company Inc.

Witmore, J. (1996) *Coaching for Performance*. 2nd edn. London: Nicholas Brealey Publishing.

Whitworth, L., Kimsey-House, H. and Sandahl, P. (1998) *Co-Active Coaching*. Palo Alto, CA: Davies-Black Publishing.

Yalom, I. (1980) *Existential Psychotherapy*. New York, NY: Basic Books.

Index

Affirmation 74–77, 99
Accreditation 12
Acknowledgement 70. 74–7, 99
Action 21, 30–31, 38, 43, 84–85, 97–98, 130, 138
  action orientation 3, 98
  action planning 28, 29, 97–98, 108, 116
Active listening 41, 64, 112
Advice giving 24
Affirmation 76–77
Appreciative inquiry 31
Association for Coaching 16

Balance wheel 139–140
Beginnings 58, 107
Beliefs 12, 18, 19, 20, 42
Berne, Eric 39
Body work 79–80
Boredom 113–114
Business Coaching 5, 124–133

Case Western University 31
Career Change 5, 11–12
Career Coaching 4, 5, 58
Carson, Richard 102
Catharsis 46
Challenging 66–70, 99, 115
Clarifying 70–75, 130, 141
Client notes 16
Coaching
  approach 4, 32, 136–137, 139–141
  client 6–7, 9
  face to face 55–8
  frame 55, 66
  language 1, 15, 48, 67, 112, 142
  package 15, 55–58, 84
  principles 36
  orientation 19, 84, 107

  process 4, 18, 19, 28, 30, 32, 41, 61, 75, 85, 97, 107, 108, 137
  relationship 15, 24, 40, Chapter 6, 107
  telephone 55–58, 114
Code of ethics 16
Cognitive-Behavioural 19–20, 43, 53, 54, 87, 120
Commitment 27, 36, 41, 49, 97
Confidentiality 16, 36, 53–54, 59–60, 127, 129–131
Confronting 66–70
Consultancy 3, 7
Contract/contracting 59–62, 107, 108, 118, 130, 132, 134
Contracting triangle 132
Cooperrider, David 31
Creative/creativity 22, 40, 42, 50, 64, 80, 96, 139
Curiosity 45, 65–66

Defence systems 20, 46, 49
Developmental disturbance 32
Difference and diversity 36
Drivers 21, 85

Ego-states 39–40
Emergent approach 88, 94
Empathy 19, 36, 41, 53, 117
Empowerment 4, 20, 88, 142
Endings 61–62, 108 (closing)
Energy 26–27, 29, 37, 40, 48, 90, 97, 111, 113, 126
European Mentoring and Coaching Council [EMCC] 16, 142
Executive coaching 4–6, 124–126
Exercises 41, 64, 75–81, 85–86, 89, 121
  affirmation 76–77

148 INDEX

body work 79–80
balance wheel 139–140
visioning 87
guided imagery [see Guided imagery]
homework 100
ideas-storming 94–96, 141
metaphor 79
paper based 76
reflective log 100

Feedback 14, 15, 70, 72–74, 110, 121, 133
Feelings 11, 23, 42–44, 61, 80, 103, 115, 120–122, 136, 138
Free association 46, 69, 92, 115
Fulfilment 19, 20, 21–23, 90
Future focus 3, 20, 38–39, 118, 141

Gestalt
  coaching 6, 135
  therapy 78
Goals 13, 21, 23, 24, 29, 38, 46, 81, 85–93, 97, 108, 112, 116, 122, 130, 141
  goal orientated 3, 135
  goal focus 20
Guided imagery 47, 75, 77–79, 103, 121, 139

Hay Julie 132
Homework 100
Holding to account 30, 98–100
Holistic 5, 34–35, 61, 126
Humanistic 19–20, 39, 45

Ideas-storming 94–96, 141
Imagination 18, 37, 40–42, 64, 78, 85, 96, 103, 121, 139
Internal saboteur 100–102, 106–107
Interrupting 68–69, 108
Interventions Chapter 5, 63, 109, 113
Intuition 65–66

Lasch, Christopher 20
Leadership Coaching 5, 129

Learning 13–15, 30–31
  cycle 30
  ladder of 13–15
Life Coaching 4–6, 124–125, 133

Making decisions 29–30
Management
  coaching 129
  practice 3, 139–141
Medical model 19, 45
Mentoring 7
Metaphor 45, 79, 112, 139
Miracle question 136
Motivation 4, 7, 12, 13, 19–20, 26, 48, 72, 88, 92, 142
Motivational interviewing 19

Negative self-talk 14, 74, 90
Neuro-linguistic programming [NLP] 78, 91
Non-content coaching 5, 84
Non-directive 4, 5, 24, 41, 112–113

Organizational Coaching 128–133

Peak experience 23, 86
Perceptions 4, 18, 19, 27, 42
Performance Coaching 4–6, 129
Person-centred 19
Personal development 3, 4, 14, 20, 31
Playfulness 22, 40
  play 36
Positive
  approach 10, 19
  development 11
  psychology 20, 31
  regard 19, 53
Possibilities 25–26, 44, 85, 93–97, 108
Potential 21, 22, 37
Powerful questions 15, 66–68, 86, 94, 141
Proactive 41, 68, 87
Professional indemnity 17
Psycho-analysis/analytical 19, 48
Psycho-emotional 7, 11, 24, 32, 37, 45, 119, 122, 135
Psychometric 15, 31, 133

INDEX

Qualification   12, 15–16
Questioning   66–70, 112, 117

Reality-testing   36, 96
Re-experiencing   46
Reflective practice   14
Reframing   27, 30, 41, 70–71, 141
Resistance   32, 48, 85, 96, 101–108, 137
Resourcefulness   37–38, 80, 141

Self-awareness   31, 133
Self-limiting beliefs   14, 27, 30, 32, 43, 48, 49, 68–69, 85, 92, 95–96, 99, 101–106, 119
Self-management   65–66
Sense of agency   21, 26–28, 48, 122
Shame   47, 49–50, 54, 60–61, 81, 99
Skill   6, 12–14, 28–29, 37, 44, 49, 64–65, 75, 76–82, 133, 139
Solutions focus   19–20, 31, 38–39, 43, 87–88, 135, 141
Speed of change   48–49
Spiritual/spirituality   34, 50–51
Stewart Ian   39
Structuring sessions   107–110
Supervision   7, 8, 14–15, 46, 54, 123

Taking responsibility   24–25
Telling and advising   8, 112, 139, 141
Transactional Analysis [TA]   39–40, 127
Transference
   co-transference   54
Transformation   13, 41–44, 88, 142
Transition   7, 41–42, 55, 126
Trauma   32
Trust   36, 47, 53–54, 64, 70, 75, 121, 127

Unconscious process   46–47, 53

Values   13, 20, 21–23, 27, 39, 85, 86, 90, 105, 122, 126
Visioning   8, 25, 87

Will   4, 26, 28–29, 92
Will power   26, 28, 92, 122
Wishes   25–26, 112
Work-based coaching   6 [see business, performance, leadership and organizational coaching]
Work/life balance   5, 18, 26, 91, 127
Working
   alliance   64, 6–70, 122
   too hard   112

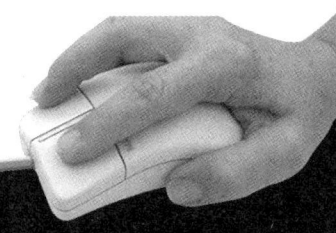